To Mother who is here in spirit

P9-DBY-752

Perfect Phrases for the Perfect Interview

Also by Carole Martin

Boost Your Interview IQ

Perfect Phrases for the Perfect Interview

Carole Martin

McGraw-Hill
New York Chicago San Francisco Lisbon
London Madrid Mexico City Milan New Delhi
San Juan Seoul Singapore Sydney Toronto

The *McGraw·Hill* Companies

Copyright © 2005 by The McGraw-Hill Companies, Inc. All rights reserved. Printed in the United States of America. Except as permitted under the United States Copyright Act of 1976, no part of this publication may be reproduced or distributed in any form or by any means, or stored in a data base or retrieval system, without the prior written permission of the publisher.

1 6 1 7 1 8 1 9 D O C / D O C 1 5 4 3 2

ISBN 0-07-144982-5

This publication is designed to provide accurate and authoritative information in regard to the subject matter covered. It is sold with the understanding that neither the author nor the publisher is engaged in rendering legal, accounting, or other professional service. If legal advice or other expert assistance is required, the services of a competent professional person should be sought.

  —From a declaration of principles jointly adopted by a Committee of the American Bar Association and a Committee of Publishers

McGraw-Hill books are available at special quantity discounts to use as premiums and sales promotions, or for use in corporate training programs. For more information, please write to the Director of Special Sales, Professional Publishing, McGraw-Hill, Two Penn Plaza, New York, NY 10121-2298. Or contact your local bookstore.

Library of Congress Cataloging-in-Publication Data
Martin, Carole.
  Perfect phrases for the perfect interview : hundreds of ready-to-use phrases that succinctly demonstrate your skills, your experience, and your value in any interview situation / Carole Martin.
    p. cm.
  Includes bibliographical references and index.
  ISBN 0-07-144982-5 (alk. paper)
1. Employment interviewing. 2. Interviewing. I. Title.
  HF5549.5.I6M37 2005
  650.14'4—dc22   2005000207

Contents

Contents

Contents

Contents

Acknowledgments

Thank you to Donya Dickerson who is the best editor around. She pushed and pulled and "we" made a great book.

An acknowledgment and thanks to everyone that I have interviewed or coached over the many years of my experience. You are the stories behind my examples and answers.

Thank you to Kathy Sparks my wonderful Virtual Assistant who is a "nag" and a wonderful caretaker.

Introduction

Words, words, words. They're everywhere. And using the right words is crucial to your success.

Words are extremely important when we are trying to sell someone on an idea or attempting to influence a decision. The most common example of using words to influence is in any type of sales transaction. Regardless of whether you have ever thought of yourself as a "sales person" or not, when you are in job search, you are in fact entering into a sales situation in which your words will be used to influence a decision. That decision will be whether the employer thinks you are the best candidate for the job.

Using the right words in the job search begins when you write your résumé. To have a successful résumé you should use the same words that employers use. These are the words that are used in postings and ads. Whether your résumé is read by an electronic résumé system or by a human résumé reader, the process will be the same—scanning for "key words." If the words are not there, you will not get the interview. The point is that it is not only important to use the "right" words and language during your job search—*it is essential!*

Introduction

This book provides you with the key words and phrases to use during your next interview, regardless of what industry you work in or what position you are interviewing for. These phrases can also be used as you write your résumé. Becoming aware of key words and knowing that the résumé reader will be seeking out these words will result in your being more focused and on track to provide the employers what they are seeking.

In this book, you will receive phrases and words to assist you in expressing yourself in the strongest way possible. You will also learn to determine "key words" for the job you are applying for, as well as the company or industry that you will be working in. By reviewing these phrases and becoming familiar with the words and phrases used to answer questions, you will find yourself expressing yourself with more confidence and will not feel as tongue tied as you may have when such questions were asked in past interviews. The more confident you feel, the stronger impression you will make during the interview. The stronger the impression you leave, the more likely you will be considered a strong contender for the job.

Part One

Getting Ready for the Interview

Chapter One

How to Use Perfect Phrases to Land Your Dream Job

The Words You Use Send a Strong Message

You are selling yourself during the entire job search process, beginning with the words you choose to write your résumé and continuing through the interview, salary negotiation, and acceptance of the offer. You are constantly revealing information about yourself and putting together a picture of yourself with words. And the words you use give details and add life and drama to your statements and stories.

Before we look at the specific phrases you can use for success, let's discuss some important ideas about choosing the best words for your interview. For starters, you should be aware of the key words used in your industry, in the companies you want to work for, and in the specific job positions you are applying for. Knowing the vocabulary for these areas is critical to your success as you interview for a specific job.

How will I know which words and phrases are "key" for the position or industry that I am applying for?

There are various sources you can look to if you want to learn words and phrases specific to your industry. You can look at company Web sites, their PR material, and even Web sites of competitors to learn what language they use. You can also look at trade magazines and journals, and even books for that industry as another resource.

Another very accessible source of key words and phrases is actually one that's *free and that can save you valuable time.* Using job boards, you can go online and look at job postings where you will discover the exact words used in the job, company, and industry. One more source to consider is the classified ads in your local newspapers, which also feature the specific job words to use. After all, experienced professionals write these words, and you can use the words to let them know you are on their wavelength and have what they are looking for. Once you become aware of these words, you will discover that there are specific words and phrases that are universal, describing what is required to succeed at specific jobs. The correct usage of these "key words" in your résumé or presentation can make or break your chances of being able to impress the interviewer and sell yourself as the best person for the job.

Some postings or ads are quite descriptive and have lots of details. Other postings will list only the essential facts. Look specifically for descriptive ads, which include a list of qualities and skills that are required in a candidate. This is considered the employer's "wish list." There is no guarantee that the words listed in the posting or description are going to be complete or that the employer won't change some of the requirements, but working with the posting will help you to plan your interview script and be prepared for whatever comes your way during the interview.

During the interview, whenever you are describing your successes and achievements, you will want to use up-to-date terms to describe your experiences and accomplishments. Words, like everything else in our lives have a "shelf life" and become old or dated. An example of using outdated words is to address a cover letter using the phrase: "To whom it may concern." While this is proper as far as grammar and protocol go, it is also very dated. This is true of industry-specific jargon as well.

Exercise

One way to prepare is to start looking at online postings, even if you aren't ready to apply for a position. Begin by visiting one of the major job boards and do an online job search. Enter the title of the job you are interested in pursuing, but at this point leave the geographical preference open. By leaving the location open, you will get a broader look at the industry and the common words and phrases that are used nationwide.

When you find job postings that are of interest to you, print them out and put them aside. After you have seven or eight, read through the postings noticing the words and phrases used. Read through the posting the first time for content. Then, read it again and begin to catch the key words used. Read the posting through one more time, but this time read between the lines. Become aware of what is *not* written. As you read between the lines, ask yourself, "What would it take to do this job?"

As you answer this question, begin writing down words that come to mind. Words such as "outgoing," "good people skills," "very organized," "good at problem solving," "flexibility" may begin to surface. Even though these words aren't written in the posting, these are the skills and traits that employers are seeking. These traits and skills are considered *transferable,* meaning that they can be taken with you from company to company, no matter the job.

Here is an example of a rather vague ad that required some reading between the lines:

> **POSTING — Customer Service Representative**
>
> Responsibilities include answering customer calls, entering orders, and processing requests. Work in a team environment. Advancement opportunity for a professional individual with outgoing personality, good communication skills, and the ability to resolve problems quickly.

This ad could be for a number of office positions that require customer contact. By reading this posting carefully, you can pick out what is written, but you can also pick up the words that are "not there." Begin to read between the lines. For example,

> **Answer customer calls**—resolve problems quickly
> (Fast-paced call center)
>
> **Good communication skills**—outgoing personality
> (Sales/customer service a plus)

Enter orders and process requests (Computer skills needed here)

Team environment (Work with others doing similar work)

Opportunity for advancement (Supervisor opportunities)

By looking beyond the actual written words and phrases and making some judgments, you can assume that this company is looking for a *very outgoing, high-energy* person to *deal with customers* who have problems—and to *do it quickly.* The person should be *computer-savvy* and have *leadership potential.*

In order to impress your interviewer, you should use the words you glean from the posting. Doing so will prove that you see what it takes to do this job—a certain type of person and you are that person! For our example, you could say:

From the job posting and our conversation during this interview, it sounds like you are seeking a person with high energy to handle customer problems with tact and diplomacy. It also seems that if the person had some computer skills and some leadership potential, you would be impressed.

You have demonstrated your ability to read between the lines and let the interviewer know that you have been listening and that you understand what it will take to do this job.

As you are interviewing, you'll want to use "perfect phrases" to show that you have these desired characteristics and that you are the perfect candidate for this job. Here's an example phrase for each of the desired skills in our example:

Energy

Perfect phrase: "If you were to ask any of my coworkers at my last job, they would tell you they call me 'Mr. Energy.' I am always upbeat with customers or co-workers."

Confidence

Perfect phrase: "I have a successful track record of working with people and solving problems quickly in a very fast-paced environment."

Great communication skills

Perfect phrase: "In my last job my customers called and asked to speak to me directly because they knew that I would take care of them while solving the problem and following through."

Ability to connect with the interviewer

Perfect phrase: "I am very interested in your company and this job. From what I have heard, it sounds like morale and team spirit run high here. That is the atmosphere where I thrive best. I feel I could bring added value to the team and to you as a manager."

Examples of past successes

Perfect phrase: "At my last job I worked in a very busy call center where I had to up-sell customers' original orders. Last quarter I increased sales 25 percent by using my unique ability to connect with customers."

By first identifying the key words and then breaking down what you think it will take to do the job, you will be able to communicate effectively about your abilities and what you can do for your customer (the employer/interviewer). This exercise also provides you with an insider's view of what the employer is looking for in the perfect candidate. The result? You'll be able to sell yourself as the ideal person for the job.

When you can sell yourself as the solution to the interviewer's problem, you will be taken seriously and stand out from the competition. Being able to stand out is especially important in a tight job market where the competition is fierce. In fact, because employers are in the driver's seat in a tight market with many candidates to choose from, they are demanding more for their money. In a normal job market employers are willing to settle for about 80 percent of the requirements they wish for. In a tight job market employers tend to be greedy and look for 100 percent of the requirements, and then some. You'll want to show that you meet their requirements, and you can do this by using the perfect phrases. By using stronger phrases than other job applicants, you'll show the interviewer through your words that you are the best person for the job.

Finding the Key Words and Phrases for Your Position

Once you have collected and printed out several job postings and descriptions—the ones with as much detail as possible— highlight or underline the words that appear more than one time. When you finish, stand back and take a look at what you've done. You will begin to see patterns as the same key words and phrases are repeated over and over. The words in the phrases may vary, but the meaning will be the same.

You will also begin to see sets of words used for specific jobs within an industry. A good way to become knowledgeable about key words and phrases is to write or collect the words that are used repeatedly. As you prepare phrases for your interview, note how often specific words are used as you go through your job search.

Keep a dictionary nearby so that when you find a word and don't understand the meaning, you can look it up before you make it "your" word. It is unwise to use a word without understanding its meaning.

Once you have formulated your list of sample words and phrases, you can review it whenever you have time. One woman conducting a job search wrote the key words and sample phrases in a small notebook and carried it with her wherever she went. When she found herself standing in long lines at places like the post office or bank, she would pull out her notebook and review her list. She was able to improve her industry vocabulary quickly by doing this. You will find that if you continue to practice these words, they will become very familiar to you and become part of your vocabulary.

The following are examples of common words and phrases found in postings for an **Executive Secretary/Admin** position.

Even though the words used are not the same, they fall into similar categories. They all came from job postings and were identified as *key* factors.

WANTED—Executive Secretary/Admin—Skills Required:

Written and oral communication skills

- "Exceptional **communication** and interpersonal skills…"
- "Strong written **communication**—grammar and composition skills…"
- "Superior oral and **written communication** skills coupled with a professional appearance…"
- "Must have strong **interpersonal and communication** skills, oral and written…"
- "Understand and be willing to work and **communicate** within **cultural protocol**…"
- "Must be **assertive**, adaptable, and able to **communicate with all levels**…"

Confidentiality—judgment

- "Ability to **handle confidential information**…"
- "Use of tact in responding to inquiries within established authority in a **confidential manner**…"
- "Handle complex or **confidential matters** requiring significant discretion and judgment…"
- "Exhibit **high level of moral and ethical behavior**; discreet…"
- "Quality, accuracy, and the ability to work without supervision **using confidentiality**…"

Self-starter

- "The ideal candidate will **work independently**—must be a **self-starter**…"
- "Must be **independent;** handle flow of communication between clients and management…"
- "Ability to work **without supervision**, confidentiality…"
- "Ability to anticipate needs/start projects **without direction** is critical…"
- "A strong sense of responsibility, initiative to problem-solve, and **work independently**…"
- "Team-oriented, flexible, with a **positive, 'can-do' attitude**…"

Prioritizing and multitasking

- "Must be able to **plan,** organize, and **follow-through**…"
- "Expected to **prioritize** and manage **multiple projects**, show initiative…"
- "Ability to handle **multiple projects simultaneously** and be detail-oriented…"
- "MUST have **excellent multitasking and proofreading** ability…"
- "Demonstrated ability **prioritizing** workload—handling **multiple tasks** simultaneously…"
- "Ability to manage **multiple** and/or **time-dependent** activities…"

Organized

- "Must be **well organized** and able to work under pressure, confidentiality required…"

■ "Needs to be a quick learner and **highly organized** with excellent follow-up skills…"
■ "Ability to take ownership of commitments and **organize/prioritize** workload…"
■ "Sense of **urgency** to understand and **meet the needs** of the team and of the organization…"

You can see by this grouping of phrases that there are certain *key phrases and words* that appear repeatedly in job postings for this position. The words and phrases vary slightly, but they are consistent in the content relating to what is needed to do the job. Note that there is an overlap in the skills desired in some phrases. Certain words appear and are coupled with other skills. For example, *well organized* and able to *work under pressure, confidentiality* required.

Using the Job Description to Prepare Your Perfect Phrases

Once you have a firm grasp of the key skills and particular experience that are required for a position, it's time to put together the phrases you will use to wow the interviewer. Let this book be your guide as you assemble the phrases you want to be sure to use in your interview.

To understand how to pick the perfect phrase, let's go back to our example: After conducting a job search for an Executive Secretary/Admin and compiling the key words and phrases, the most common words/phrases were identified as the following:

■ Written and oral communication skills
■ Confidentiality and judgment

- Self-starter—independent
- Prioritizing and multitasking
- Very organized

Using the Executive Secretary/Admin position, you can see how effective it is to summarize what you have found to be the key words for the interview.

Perfect Phrase:

"From what I have read in your job posting, it appears that you want someone who has superior communications skills, both written and oral. It sounds like it would take someone who can work independently and who is a self-starter. That matches with my skills completely."

You have demonstrated an ability to summarize and "cut to the chase" by getting directly to what you believe it would take to do this job. Your use of terms and phrases also shows a grasp of the job requirements and excellent communication skills. Whenever you say, "It sounds like…" you are paraphrasing what you have just heard or read. This is a communication skill that will take you far. It is letting the person with the problem know that you understand his or her problem.

Perfect Phrase:

"I believe my past experiences as an Exec Administrator would make me a perfect fit for this job. One of the qualities I have that I pride myself in is my ability to protect information, particularly confidential information. My last boss would tell you he trusted me with his personal information as well as his top-secret business information."

Since confidentiality is high on the list of requirements for an Executive Secretary/Admin, you have let the interviewer know that this is something you excel in. Using a quote or paraphrasing what your last boss would say is another way of letting the interviewer know something about you without actually saying it yourself. By saying, "My boss would say, ..." you are using a third-party endorsement to make your statement strong.

Perfect Phrase:

"I can see that someone who is organized and able to prioritize and who works well under pressure while multitasking is your ideal candidate. I will remind you that these are my strengths, as proven by my past experiences in similar situations. From what I hear and see, I am the perfect candidate for your job. I am someone who can make your business life easier."

Another opportunity to tell the interviewer that you know what it takes to do this job and that you have "been there and done that." You have also let the interviewer know that you believe in your ability, and you also make an offer that would be tempting to any boss, "I can make your business life easier."

By actually mentioning the skills in your answers, you let the interviewer see that you have an idea of their importance and that you understand what it will take to get this job done. Doing this will improve your chances of both connecting with the interviewer and being remembered as someone who "gets the point. " You have also let the interviewer know that you are the "perfect candidate" for the position by relaying your strengths and past experiences. Well done!

Giving the perfect answer in your interview is easier than you think. When you can identify the key skills and speak about the requirements of the job using key words and phrases, you will sound polished and knowledgeable about what the employer/interviewer is seeking. You can also sell yourself with more confidence if you know that you have the required skills necessary to do the job and that you have something to offer. You have what the employer is looking for!

Top Eight Word Mistakes Candidates Make in Job Interviews

1. Use language that is too informal

It is important to remember that you are interviewing for a job, not trying to make a new best friend. Too much familiarity can hurt your chances by making you look unprofessional.

> **Poor Phrase:** "I'm sure **you guys** are aware that the job market is **in the dumps** right now. It's been **one heck of an uphill battle** for me for the past year."

> **Perfect Phrase**: "Unfortunately, as I am sure you are aware, the job market is still tight, and there is a great deal of heavy competition for the same jobs."

2. The use of words that are vague

Words such as "a lot," "various/multiple," and "great deal of" are vague and don't give the interviewer the needed information.

> **Poor Phrase:** "I have had **a lot of experience** with **various lines of multiple** products. I am proud of the results I've had in saving the company a **great deal of money**."

> **Perfect Phrase:** "With over eight years experience working in the paper industry and primarily selling photo paper, I consider myself an expert on the subject and have saved my clients as much as 20 percent on orders over $5000."

3. Misuse of pronouns

It can be very confusing and words can be misinterpreted when pronouns are misused. Be especially alert to this when you are using the pronouns "we," "I," and "you."

> **Poor Phrase:** "**We** were behind on **our** project, and **we** decided that **we** would stay and finish the job rather than miss **our** deadline. **We** pulled it together, and **we** were able to meet **our** deadline."

> **Perfect Phrase:** "I worked with a team of designers to bring a project in on time. We each took responsibility for a particular area. We worked closely, but at the same

time we were completely disconnected from one another. This seemed to work because my four counterparts and I managed to pull the project together on time."

4. Using company-specific words

Each company has certain terms that are indigenous only to that company. Outsiders will not know what you are talking about if you use these terms. This is especially true if you have worked for a public organization or the military. You should use as many specific words as possible in your interview so that the hiring manager knows you are familiar with your industry.

> **Poor Phrase:** "While I was working on **the 767 project**, I discovered an error in the "**Whichamaculit**" used to produce our **656 product line**. This was a really costly mistake."

> **Perfect Phrase:** "At my last company there was a particular marketing project that involved a software conversion. Because of my strong attention to detail, I was able to catch an error that would have cost the company millions of dollars."

5. Assuming everyone knows the acronym you are using

Acronyms are used at every company—shortcuts used internally to eliminate a lot of words. Avoid using these in an interview because the hiring manager may not be familiar with the acronyms used at your current company.

> **Poor Phrase:** "I was considered an **SAR** and supported three **line reps** who were in the **SWSC area**."

> **Perfect Phrase:** "My position title was sales associate representative, and I supported the sales representatives who were responsible for the southwest area of South Carolina."

6. Describing skills by using "weak" words

Beware of small words that can sabotage your credibility— words like "pretty," "most of the time," and "kind of."

> **Poor Phrase:** "I'm **pretty good** with computers—**at least most of the time** I am. I **kind of taught** myself most of the programs."

> **Perfect Phrase:** "I am very knowledgeable about Unix software. When I was unfamiliar with programs in the past, I taught myself in less than two weeks. I am a very quick learner."

7. Use too few words to answer the question

One pet peeve many interviewers have is not getting enough information. When a candidate answers a question with one or two words, it's impossible to make a judgment as to whether this person is the right person for the job.

> **Poor Phrase:** "Yes, I have had experience in that area."

> **Perfect Phrase:** "I have over 10 years working with biotech testing. If you were to ask any of my coworkers, they would tell you that I hold the record for the least number of mistakes when using testing equipment."

8. Talking too much—not getting to the point

When you fail to prepare for the interview, you can easily ramble and go off the subject down some other road. A rule of thumb is, **"Your answers should be no longer than two to three minutes long."**

> **Poor Phrase:** "My last company has developed software to support government enforcement of firearms violators. This nationwide project will be the first of its kind and will allow users to investigate firearms traffickers and purchasers. The software is able to track violent offenders and unscrupulous federal firearms licensees. This product will allow users to investigate and prosecute violators and felons by tracking their activities from remote locations. The product has been developed in cooperation with the U.S. government and will hopefully be purchased and used by all branches of law enforcement agencies that could use this tracking method. The company has invested over

two years in developing and perfecting this product and has invested a great percentage of the company's revenue in it, betting that this is going to have a big payoff long term. Short term it has put a considerable squeeze on the finances needed to run everyday work projects. If it is successful, it will be a huge coup for those who have hung in there. If it is not successful, it will be a huge loss to the company and will probably result in massive layoffs. So the whole project is going to make or break the company and it's future."

Perfect Phrase: "At my last company I served as lead in getting a new tracking product launched nationwide. The product will be used to track firearms violators and bring them to conviction through evidence collected. I worked closely with the U.S. government and followed the regulations necessary to develop such a product."

Preparing for Follow-Up Questions

As you put together your phrases, always try to think of any follow-up questions you might be asked. Of course, you would never use a word or say a phrase just to impress your interviewer without knowing the definition behind the word. You should also never use a phrase unless you have an example to back up the word or phrase. When you can communicate to the interviewer a specific example regarding skills you used in the past, you will have a better chance of convincing him or her that you are knowledgeable about the subject you are describing.

Example

A young man might say during an interview, "I have excellent written and oral communication skills." The interviewer could follow-up with a question like, "Can you give me an example of a time when you used your written communication skills?" The candidate might look embarrassed if he didn't have an example. He said that he had great written communication skills because he thought it sounded good.

Exercise for Preparing for Follow-Up Questions

Here's a simple exercise that will help you prepare for follow-up questions. It will also help you take a look inside yourself and begin to think about what you want more of, and what you want less of, in your next job. People usually perform at a higher level if they are satisfied with the work they do and are, therefore, motivated to give 100 percent plus.

Start by making a list of the responsibilities and tasks you performed at your last job. These would be the projects or tasks that you were particularly proud of or were energized by. Think about the last time you were so involved in a project or task that you woke up thinking about how you could improve the situation. Write those experiences down and try to determine what the factors were that were satisfying for you.

Let's say you were a project leader. The tasks list would read something like: "Led a team; coordinated and monitored project progress; ensured the flow and completion of work on schedule; monitored expenditures and budget." Now you have solid examples of your skills that you can use for any follow-up question.

After you have written this list for your most current job, try doing the same thinking for previous jobs. If you recently graduated from college, use the classes that were most stimulating and interesting for you or the projects you worked on with teams when you were in school.

By making lists of motivating experiences from your last two or three jobs, you will begin to notice patterns of projects and tasks that stand out. Analyze what those tasks involved. Do you want more or less of this type of responsibility in your next job? The answer will tell you what you want and may suggest some possibilities for fulfillment in future jobs that have similar responsibilities. Knowing what you want will make you feel more confident about finding the right job.

Getting Ready for Success

This book provides you with the phrases you need for success. Use the phrases in this book as building blocks for your own phrases. They will give you the competitive edge.

These perfect phrases are to be used as a guide or template to assist you in using effective wording to express yourself. You may find that seeing examples will give you ideas for your own stories. Forming your own phrases using these guides will make your statements stronger. It would be unwise to use them as "cookie cutter" answers unless the answer matches what you actually did. A good rule is to use these phrases but to never say anything that you don't have an example of a time when you actually had the experience.

Armed with your perfect phrases, you will feel confident going into any interview situation, and you will be sure to wow any interviewer. Now, let's get to the phrases!

Part Two

**Perfect Phrases for
the Perfect Interview:
General Questions**

Chapter Two

Who You Are and What You Know

The purpose of any interview is to give the interviewer an accurate picture of you. The interviewer wants to know what makes you unique and where you've been on your career path. Using appropriate words and phrases will assist you in getting the necessary information across. This chapter focuses on the topics of you and your knowledge, providing you with words and phrases to help you create an accurate picture for the interviewer.

Breaking the Ice

"Did you find the place okay?"

- "Yes, and I actually had extra time to catch a cup of coffee across the street. Thanks for the great directions. The route that you advised me to take saved me a lot of time and helped me to avoid some heavy traffic."

- "I'm one of those people who plans ahead. I actually took a dry-run drive last week to make sure I knew where I was going. I really dislike the idea of being late—especially for an interview."

- "I took a couple of wrong turns, but I don't ever let mistakes throw me. I just turned around and went back. Luckily I had allowed extra time, so I was not upset when I got lost. Eventually I figured it out and arrived in plenty of time."

"How was your commute?"

- "You know how traffic can be. I used your directions and also listened to the traffic reports on the radio. I was able to avoid a couple of trouble spots."

- "Because I left early, it was very relaxing. I always allow extra time when I have appointments. I learned that lesson when I got a flat tire and hadn't allowed extra time in case of the unexpected. Unfortunately I was late to an important appointment. I've never been late since that incident."

- "I took public transportation in and took the earlier train to allow me time to walk the few blocks to get here. I am an avid walker. I stay in shape by walking whenever I can."

"How was your trip here?"

- "Other than a four hour delay with my connecting flight, it was fine. I'm sure you have travel experience in today's skies and know the routine. I have learned to always fly with a good book—just in case."

- "Because travel is such a big part of my job as a sales rep, I am used to schlepping and waiting. If you aren't going to be flexible and relaxed about changes and delays, you are going to experience a lot of grief while traveling. I love traveling and experiencing new places."

- "My trip in was great. I took the train instead of flying. I find trains more relaxing. I was able to read a few business magazines on the trip. I read some interesting reports about one of your competitors in today's business section. Did you know that XYZ Company was being bought out by ABC?"

"How is your summer going so far?"

- "Right now my job search is taking up most of my time. I am spending at least six to eight hours a day working on leads and networking. I have been able to get away for a couple of weekends, and that was really relaxing. How about yours?"

- "Summer seems to be flying by. I don't know where the weeks have gone. I took one week at the beginning of the summer to go to visit relatives in California, but since then I have been really busy at work. How about you? Have you been able to take any time off?"

- "It's been going great so far. I have been taking time off from my job search one day a week and going somewhere that I typically don't go during the week. I really find it delightful because it is less crowded. It would be a real luxury to work four days a week; unfortunately I can't afford that luxury."

"Cold enough for you?"

- "I'm one of those unusual persons who enjoys cold. I guess it brings back good memories of skiing and spending time outdoors in the snow."
- "I have to admit that winter is not my favorite time of the year. But wearing the right clothes makes a big difference. The first year that I moved here I invested in a good, warm topcoat."
- "Weather is not a big deal for me. I just adjust to whatever climate I happen to live in. I moved around a lot as a kid and got used to dealing with whatever was out there."

"Tell me about yourself."

- "For the past six years I have been in the electronics industry working on computer systems. I take an analytical view of what is happening and work through the process by trying various solutions. I work well independently or as a member of a team. I have worked in fast-paced environments most of my life and am very goal-oriented and deadline-driven."

- "I have over four years experience as a technician. Two years ago I was promoted to lead technician, and I currently supervise four testers and technicians. My strength is problem solving. I do whatever it takes to get the problem solved as quickly and efficiently as possible."

- "I am a person who enjoys problem solving. For the past six years I have been working on projects and problems involving software design. In my last position I was able to solve a design problem that had been around for a while. As a result, the company was able to sell a product that had been delayed for some time to our biggest customer."

"Are you familiar with our company?"

- "My research has turned up quite a bit of information about your company and its founders. I was very impressed by the background of your two founders. I was also very interested to read several articles in journals about the latest research your company is conducting."

- "I've known of your company for the last couple of years. I happened to see an article in the paper about some funding that you were obtaining from an investment group, and this drew my interest because of my background in the field. I think what your company is working on is very cutting edge and something that I want to be a part of."
- "I went to your Web site and was impressed by all the products and services your company provides. I had no idea that your company had the extensive reach that it has. I also read some articles online that pertained to your latest products."

"How would you describe yourself?"

- "I would say that I am knowledgeable about computer programs and that I have a strong ability to solve problems. Also I stay focused and on track when I am working on a project."
- "I'd describe myself as a person who is upbeat. I try not to let little things in life get to me. I'm known for my positive attitude at work. I'm also looked to for information. People know that they can come to me with their problems and that I will listen and try to do what I can to solve them."
- "Anybody who has ever worked with me would tell you that I am a fun person to be around. I also know when to be serious and when it is important to be focused on what I am doing. I think I am a balanced person who enjoys my work and my surroundings."

"What are three words that describe you?"

- "'Hard working' is the first. Anyone I work with would tell you that I do whatever it takes to get the job done. Second is 'team player' because I thrive in environments that are supportive and collaborative. And last, 'knowledgeable regarding accounting information.' Through my education and my experience I have a strong background in all phases of accounting."

- "'Reliable.' I never miss deadlines. 'Friendly.' I have an upbeat attitude. And 'thorough.' I always try to get it right the first time."

- "The first would be 'expert' on the subject of mainframes. Second would be 'communicator,' because I talk to everyone I come in contact with. Third would be 'organized,' because I am a planner and always have a schedule planned out."

Past Experiences

"What experience do you have that qualifies you for this job?"

- "I have a total of ten years experience, with the majority of my experience in teaching. When I read the job posting, I felt confident that I would be qualified and could bring added value to this job, particularly in the area of curriculum development."

- "I provided technical problem resolution and ensured effective coordination of activities in every job that I have held. I have also gained a reputation within the manufacturing industry as a key player when it comes to hard bargaining and negotiations. In my last two jobs I was able to save the companies thousands of dollars by negotiating savvy business deals."

- "First, my excellent communication skills and my ability to work with all types of people. This is important because of the interaction within various departments involved in projects. Next, I am very organized with strong coordination skills. It takes the ability to prioritize and to be adaptable in order to succeed in this type of position. Last are my strong coordinating skills that are necessary to keep on track and on schedule."

Why do you think you are a good match for this job?

- "My years of experience in this industry make me feel confident that I can do this job and bring added value. I am extremely knowledgeable about your customer base and your competitors and what it will take to sell your newer products. I am also very well connected in this industry and therefore can be very resourceful." "If you asked any of my coworkers at my last job, they would tell you that 'I am good with people, conscientious about my reports, and very organized.' From what I've read about this position, that more than qualifies me as a good match for this job."

- "I'm a person who is passionate about what I do. I am fortunate that I have found work where I can help people have better lives. Nothing gives me more pleasure than to help someone move out of a bad situation and find a new direction."

What makes you think that you can do this job?

- "When I compared your requirements with my qualifications, I found that they were a very good match. You are looking for six years experience, and I have over six years of experience selling a comparable product. You are looking for someone with excellent communication skills, and I have a track record of selling to some of the most difficult people in the industry."
- "My six years of experience in sales plus my MBA provide me with the perfect skill set that you are seeking. I have a proven record of being top performer in my company for the past two years. I know I have what it takes to do this job."
- "I have a strong working relationship with all the manufacturing people as well as the union representatives. As the liaison I can head off problems that might flare before it is too late."

Career Goals

"What are your short-term and long-term goals?"

- "My career path is not set in stone. One thing I have learned is to stay flexible to opportunities. I have read your literature and visited your Web site, and know that there are open opportunities with someone with my background and education. I know that whatever I do, I will continue to take on additional responsibilities and challenges."
- "My short-term goal is to find a job in a company where I can bring value to the team. My longer-term goal is to continue to take classes in the evening in management and eventually manage projects."
- "My last company was my first job out of college, and I've come a long way in experience there. But now my goal is to join a larger company that has career opportunities and programs for development. I have researched such companies, and I know that this company believes in career development for its employees. My longer-term goals are flexible, depending on the career path I establish in the new company."

"What goals have you set for yourself in your career?"

- "I am very goal-oriented and have completed all the goals I have set for myself in past jobs. My long-term goal is to become a specialist in the field of IT management."
- "When I look at goals, I like to remain somewhat flexible. I have found that the world is changing so rapidly that it is not a good idea to lock oneself into specific goals that may not be achievable. I do know that I want to continue

to advance and become more and more of an expert in my field. I would eventually like to take on more responsibility as a project or product manager."

- "I am looking beyond what I do at my current company and want to advance when I am ready and someday move into a management position. From what I know about this company and your vision for employees, it is exactly the company that I am looking to join. I know it will take time and hard work, but I am ready and willing to do whatever it takes."

"How do you see our company helping you achieve your goals?"

- "I've done extensive research on the kind of company that I want to be affiliated with so that I can achieve my career goals. Your company is among the top five companies that I have set my sights on. I believe the values of this company are very much in line with the values that I have set for myself."

- "I have been aware of the progress and growth this company has made over the past four years while I have been earning my Bachelor's degree. In fact, I did a case study as one of my assignments in college using your company as a model of steady growth. The career development program your company offers is of special interest to me."

- "I see this company as one that values its employees and the contributions that employees have to make. I have had several friends who have worked here, and they have shared some great employer stories with me. I know this is a company where I could work collaboratively with bright people to achieve my goals."

"What industry experience do you have that qualifies you to do this job?"

- "My knowledge and experience in this industry encompasses a total of 10 years. I see real value in my years of experience with a company that has similar customers and contacts. I have built strong relationships throughout my career that will help me hit the ground running at this company."

- "I consider myself an expert in the field of data mining. As you can see from my résumé, I have worked nationally and internationally as a consultant. I have worked with Fortune 500 companies as well as small start-ups. I have a broad scope of experience and expertise to pull from to analyze and solve problems of a broad scope."

- "I've been interested in working for your company for some time. I have extensive experience in the fashion industry and know that sales are on the soft side right now because of economic conditions. I also know that you have a new product set to launch by the end of the year. I am interested in becoming a key contributor. I want to be part of the team that makes this company a stronger contender in today's challenging market."

"What can you bring to this job from your previous experience?"

- "My extensive experience and educational background qualify me as an expert. My wide range of experiences in both the education system as well as the business sector allow me to have a broader view of how a school system can be run like a business. My past success and accomplishments speak for the value I can bring to this type of position."

- "I have made some long-lasting relationships with customers by building rapport through trust. I pride myself on my customer service skills, including follow-through and experience. I am very thorough, with strong attention to detail. I enjoy thinking 'outside the box' and coming up with new ways to look at old problems—either on my own or as a team member."

- "My successes in customer service have made me one of the top producers in my company. I have customers who ask for me specifically when they have problems because they know that I will listen and do whatever I can to resolve the situation."

"How does this job compare and contrast with what you have done in the past?"

- "This job is very similar in that I would be selling to a similar customer base. The contrast would be the nature of the product and your company's reputation in standing behind the product. I believe that, armed with these additional tools, I can bring very good results to the territory and company."

- "The company is different and the product is new, but I know I have what it takes to do this job. In my last position within two months of being hired I was on the top-performer list."

■ "The job I was performing in my last company was almost a perfect match with this job. I really loved that job and was sorry when I was laid off. The company went through many changes, and eventually my job was affected. What I liked most about the job was that I worked in a team environment with some really great people. I know that this job has a similar team environment, and that's why I'm interested in pursuing the opportunity."

"What experience do you have that matches the requirements of this job?"

- "I have a proven record building strong relationships with key customers that have resulted in increased revenue for the company. From reading through your job posting, I believe that this is exactly the experience and record you are seeking in a job candidate."
- "I have been successful in achieving premium service on a shoestring budget. I received an achievement award last year for producing results in a market that was all but dead."
- "I consider myself an expert in the field of data mining, as you can see from my résumé, I have worked nationally and internationally as a consultant. I have worked with Fortune 500 companies as well as small start-ups. My experience and expertise allow me to analyze and solve problems of a broad scope."

"What would your boss say about your performance in your last position?"

- "My boss would give me the highest praise. He would say that my achievements and my thorough understanding of mergers and acquisitions have made me an invaluable member of the M&A team."
- "She would tell you that I have exceeded all my goals for the past two years. She manages me from an off-site location and depends on me to manage my area independently. We have a very trusting relationship, and she would tell you that I have always been reliable and

dependable. She would also tell you that I have built great relationships with internal customers."

- "He would be sure to tell you that I stay current and abreast of the latest changes in the field. That's one of my strengths. I like research and knowledge, and everyone knows that they can come to me for answers to questions on current rules and regulations."

"Tell me about a time when your knowledge of your position made a difference in the outcome of a situation."

- "Because I have such strong planning and coordinating experience, I was able to put together a conference for 500 people that ran very smoothly. I planned the event by starting with a venue that would accommodate that large an audience. I had a committee who I worked with and directed. Each person on the committee was in charge of a segment of the conference—invitations, catering, and entertainment. I used an Excel spreadsheet to track the scheduling and events. We all worked very long and hard, but the results were an extremely successful conference with very positive feedback."

- "During a threatened union strike by our hospital workers, my ability to work with diverse people, plus my negotiating skills, was the key factor in working out a resolution so that the strike never happened. Needless to say, management commended me on my skilled dealings with the workers and my ability to listen to them and work through their issues with the managers."

- "I am very knowledgeable about Unix systems and recently worked on a server for a large facility that had 500-plus employees. I provided Unix support to all divisions, including maintenance of hardware and software on several workstations. I was able to ensure daily backups of software and research data. I also updated the operating systems with the latest upgrades and created accounts for new users. The project was done in record time and continues to run smoothly with minimum maintenance."

"What do you consider your strengths?"

- "I have several strengths I can bring to this job. First of all my background—experience and education—are a perfect fit for this position. Second, I have excellent written and oral communication skills. And last, I am very flexible and adaptable to new situations."

- "One of the strongest points is my ability to work with a diversity of people. Regardless of the situation, I have the ability to adapt and work under any circumstances. In my last job I worked in a small room with 13 people all speaking various languages, and still managed to stay focused."

- "My strength is my ability to remain calm in chaotic situations. I have had to keep my cool in every job I have ever held. Fast-paced environments are no longer a challenge to me; they are a way of life. I manage to stay centered no matter what is happening, and as a result the people around me feel calmer."

"What skill has been praised or rewarded in your past jobs?"

- "I have an outstanding record of error-free calculations for my customers. When it comes to money, people don't like mistakes. I pride myself on my ability to be very detail-oriented when it comes to figures."

- "A major strength of mine is my ability to forecast expenditures for budget planning. This has been very important in my success and has kept various managers within their spending limits."

- "I am a proven performer when it comes to connecting with doctors and getting them to recommend my products to patients. As for my appraisals, I have always been a high achiever no matter where I have worked."

"What skills can you bring from your previous jobs?"

- "I have worked effectively in three different industries and have been able to make the transition with minimum downtime. My ability to learn quickly and 'hit the ground running,' has made a huge impact on my career."
- "One of the skills that I take pride in is my ability to listen to people and really hear what they say. I consider this to be key in sales. Before I even think of selling someone something, I find out what the needs are."
- "My key strengths are my strong analytical skills and my ability to use those skills to see all sides of a problem. Problem solving is my strength and greatest asset."

"Give me an example of a time when you used your strength to achieve results."

- "My strength as an employee is my dependability. There was a situation in which I was on call to cover any computer disasters over the weekend. A call came in, and I was not the technician closest to the company involved but I could see that no one else was responding. I had weekend plans but considered my job first. I responded to the call four hours before anyone else and was able to prevent downtime for the company on Monday morning."
- "Working for an executive who was out of town a great deal of time, I often made decisions based on my judgment. There was one incident when I had to make a

decision about calling a meeting off or trying to get someone else to cover the meeting for my boss in his absence. I made a few critical calls and was able to avoid canceling a meeting that would have involved out-of-town executives. Everyone, including my boss, was grateful for my quick thinking and judgment."

- "My knowledge of construction and the laws and regulations—county, state, and federal—saved one company that I worked for a great deal of money. Working as a consultant, I was able to see that one project was in danger of violating several building codes. I was able to make suggestions to bring the project to code and as a result saved the company money in building costs and as well as fines."

Uniqueness

"What makes you unique?"

- "Not only am I a successful manager, but I worked my way up from the bottom position in the company to get there."
- "If you were to ask any of my colleagues, they would tell you that I am known for my unique ability to get people to do things for me without asking directly."
- "What makes me unique is that my outside interest is playing the piano and my 'day job' is working on the computer all day long. So I am constantly playing with sets of keys."

"Tell me about a time when you solved a problem in a unique manner."

- "As a publicist, one of the challenges of my job is to think of unique ideas to promote my client or product. There was one publicity campaign I handled for a product that we called a 'real knock out.' I purchased hundreds of key chains with small boxing gloves attached and sent them as part of the press kit to radio and television studios. It was unique, so it drew attention and got great results for my client."
- "An engineering project I worked on at my last company saved over $1 million in operating costs. I created, published, and implemented a unique plan for underwater storage. I was in charge of implementation, and, because of my planning and coordination of departments, it was a great success."
- "I was given the challenging task of continuing our community educational programs, but with a more limited budget than in previous years. The first thing I did was to apply for grant money. Then I put together an

47

aggressive volunteer program. Because of my ability to come up with new ideas, we were able to continue our classes, seminars, and workshops in a seamless manner without raising the costs of the classes."

"Give me an example of how your uniqueness has helped you in your work."

- "I'm known for my ability to 'think outside the box.' I came up with an original idea to raise funds for the police children's annual toy drive. I contracted with the local movie theater to give a free movie ticket to every person who brought in a toy over the cost of $5. The results were like none we've ever had before. We had a record contribution, and the donors received a gift in return. It was a very successful year."

- "It was when I was a student. I used a unique way to get around campus and the city; I rollerskate everywhere. I figured I was getting more exercise skating than I would get walking. I didn't have time to exercise, so I kept fit by using this method to commute. I was also able to listen to my class tapes while I skated. It was a great way to get around and study at the same time."

- "The unique part of this example is that I was able to lead a cross-functional team in a company that had never used cross-functional teams before. As the lead engineer I decided to try an experiment, and took people from various functions and cross-trained them. We were able to do twice the design, testing, and production in a shorter period and saved the company money in the process. It was received well and is now a common practice at the company."

Chapter Three

Skills Set

Sometimes when we are asked what our strengths are, we tend to think "knowledge-based skills." These are the skills you've acquired from experience and education. While these skills are important, the next person to be interviewed may be equally qualified in these skills. There are two other categories that are very important when you are trying to establishing your uniqueness in interviews. These are your transferable skills and your personal traits.

- **Knowledge-based skills** are skills learned through experience or education, such as computer programs, graphics, languages, and writing
- **Transferable skills** are portable—you can take them with you to almost any job. Examples are communication, listening, decision-making, judgment, initiative, planning, and organizing. Chances are that you are probably taking for granted some of the skills that make you unique.
- **Personal traits** are qualities that make you who you are— flexibility, integrity, friendliness, dependability, good attitude. These skills cannot be taught, even though some

employers would like to teach them, and they should be valued as important.

When you are trying to establish what makes you unique, think of all three categories and where you want to focus to let the interviewer know that you are the best person for the job and why.

Creativity

"What experience can you bring that involved creativity?"

- "I pride myself on my ability to look at all aspects of a problem. I have come up with some very original solutions to problems that no one else seemed able to solve. I have always been known for my ability to think 'outside the box.'"

- "I have had a full range of experience in the film industry, working with lighting and cameras. I have worked on last minute deadlines where there were problems to solve, and I solved them using lots of resourcefulness. I not only met the deadlines and goals, but I thrived in those situtations. It was when my creative juices were flowing at their best"

- "My design and layout experience runs the full range from producing newsletters to major publications. Every year for the past four years I have received the award for the most creative format for my newsletters."

"Tell me about a time you used creativity in your current (last) position?"

- "My latest project involves coordinating an ad campaign for our company. I am working with an agency, but some of the time I have found their ideas to be trite. I have jumped in and offered some 'off-the-wall' ideas to get their juices flowing. It has worked, and we are heading into the home stretch on one of the most creative projects I have ever seen at my company."

- "My job is usually not very creative, since I'm working with systems. But there was a project when I had to solve a problem for a customer that was way out of the ordinary.

The customer wanted to make the system do something that was possible but not the usual way of doing things. I worked with him through numerous phone calls and emails, and together we were able to override the system and accomplish what he wanted. He was thrilled with my efforts—above and beyond the norm. He actually called my boss to tell him about my efforts and told him that I had great customer service skills. That was a wonderful experience for me."

- "One of my latest accomplishments was composing and compiling a procedures manual for the biotechnology department in the company I worked for as a consultant. There was no manual in place, and so it entailed interviewing many of the employees from the top-ranking officials to the administrative personnel in order for me to get a sense of what had been used as procedures to that point. I was able to use the general operating practices as a guide for writing the manual so that it wasn't a drastic change from what had been going on. It turned out very well, and the users were satisfied with the results."

"The position requires a lot of outside-the-box thinking. How comfortable are you with thinking creatively on your feet?"

- "I am not only comfortable but very experienced in thinking outside-the-box. Because I work with so many customers, I have to be highly adaptable to their needs. I remember one customer came into the office and wanted to watch production of her product. This is highly unusual and dangerous. I decided that a way she could view the live production was on camera. I set up a video camera, and she sat in the office next door to production. She could see live work and still be within the safety codes. She was satisfied and felt that we had accommodated her needs."

- "If you were to ask any of my coworkers, they would tell you that I am known for my outside-the-box solutions. In fact, I recently helped one of our workers' son build a racing vehicle for an amateur race he will be competing in. No one else could think of a way to make his vehicle unique. I came up with a design that was unheard of, and he won a prize for most unusual design."

- "My boss accused me of majoring in creativity in college. I have this ability to see a problem from all directions and then to apply some of my unique thinking to come up with outside-the-box solutions. I watched a production line operate one time and could envision a whole new way that the process could be run with fewer people and more efficiently. I sold my idea to the foreman, and he implemented it as soon as he was able. I got an award for thinking uniquely that time."

Communications

"How would you describe your communication style?"

- "I possess superior customer service skills that have allowed me to build a solid reputation as being trustworthy and honest in my dealings."
- "I have the ability to break down very complex technical terms into everyday, simple language for the nontechnical person to understand. This allows me to communicate with a broad range of people to get a task completed."
- "My excellent listening skills allow me to hear much more than most people hear. Using my intense listening skills and then letting the person know that I 'heard' him or her has made a tremendous difference in working with people at all levels within the organization."

"Tell me about a time when your communication style made a difference in a project."

- "I was the key contact during this year's labor negotiations of the new contract. As the liaison between labor and management, I was able to be objective and let each side know that I heard its issues. I was then able to suggest a compromise. Because both sides saw that I was being open and objective, they trusted me and talked to me openly. In the end we were able to satisfy both sides."
- "I am an experienced presenter and often present to groups of major decision makers. There was a particular time that I presented to key decision makers in a multi-million dollar investment firm. By finding out what its expectations and needs were in the beginning and

letting people there know that I understood their expectations, I was able to influence them into buying our entire system."

■ "My writing ability has allowed me to present the facts, but it also gives me an opportunity to present ideas within my own framework. I worked with a team of graphic designers to create the Web site for our company. Although the design was very important, the words I wrote blended to make a complete and important message. The site has been recognized as one of the top Web sites in the industry."

"Can you give me an example of a major project you worked on that involved communication and writing?"

■ "Last year I was put in charge of developing a monthly newsletter for the administrative support types in the company. This was my first experience at putting together a publication from start to finish. The first thing I did was consult with people in the company who had written similar publications. From what they told me, I was able to get a sense of what people liked and didn't like. I interviewed everyone from the guys in the mailroom to the CEO and wrote articles about them. I also came up with a clever format that included a writing contest with a prize for the best story. The best part was that people got their story published in the next edition of the newsletter. My idea really sparked a lot of interest and enthusiasm and allowed me to share the writing with others. The newsletter was a big success among the intended audience. I even received an award for the best internal newsletter."

- "A large part of my job as a public relations consultant involves writing media material. There was one project where the company was sponsoring a major spring event as an outreach to the community. I wrote the press releases, public service announcements, radio ads, and even the speeches for key management presentations. The writing project was in addition to coordinating the volunteers as well as the hired vendors such as the caterer and sound technicians. I was really involved in every aspect of the event. It was a huge project that turned out well all around."

- "There was a major project in which I authored seven proposals that secured seven contracts worth over $1 million. I wrote the proposals with tight deadlines that I had to honor. I supervised the field technicians and subcontractors to bring those projects in on time with a 25 percent profit margin. Needless to say, I was rewarded highly for that accomplishment."

Strategic Thinking

"Tell me about using strategic thinking in your current job."

- "I have led the strategic planning team for my company, which has successfully generated $3 million over the last quarter."
- "My responsibilities have encompassed long-range strategic planning and product development. I've worked with a diverse team and have come up with plans that have been extremely successful."
- "I'm a key member of the strategic planning committee. We implemented a state-of-the-art information system to automate core business. This was met with great enthusiasm and support."

"Can you give me an example of a time when strategic thinking made a difference in a project you worked on?"

- "At my last company I developed a strategic plan that reduced payroll costs by 8 percent in the first year. It involved developing and implementing ongoing efficiency training.
- "While working with a strategic planning team, I was the originator of the idea to completely change our Web site sales strategy to be more interactive. The idea was met with great enthusiasm by the team and when it rolled out some months later, I was given credit for the idea."
- "Through strategic planning my team was able to turn around a loss to 20 percent ROI within six months. By planning and forecasting we were able to control the process that led to the increase."

"Give me an example of your using strategic thinking at work."

- "I worked on a manufacturing project, performing technology programming and support. I developed data models and procedures to convert a training administration system to new software. I also administered data security for the system."

- "I worked on a cost reduction program that entailed developing and implementing a long-range capital improvement purchase plan. I came up with the idea to subcontract and consolidate facilities while increasing machine utilization by 30 percent. Through these cost-saving measures we were able to stay within budgetary restraints and still make a profit."

- "We had a problem with one of our computer systems. The first step I take when solving any problem is to do as much research as possible to define the problem. In this particular case it was a problem with the mainframe. I consulted with the IT department and the systems engineers to tap their resources to help to fix the problem. Based on the research and recommendations of the 'experts,' I put together a plan to attack the problem and then moved into action, and I was able to retrace the breakdown. I kept in constant communication with the IT department until we had the problem solved. We did this with a minimum of downtime."

Assertiveness

"How would you describe your assertiveness?"

- "I have been able to step up to the plate on more than one occasion when no one else would lead a project. I guess you could consider that initiative as well. When I see that there is a problem and that I can solve that problem, I move forward. I am careful to work with the team if that is the situation that I am in."

- "My open communication style has allowed me to be assertive on several occasions when things became tense among employees or when there was a problem between another employee and me. I firmly believe that talking something through in a nonconfrontational style is the best solution most of the time."

- "At my last company I was promoted to lead person because of my ability to speak up when I saw a problem and to suggest a solution whenever I had one. I have learned to speak up when I see a more efficient way of doing things, as long as I am not stepping on someone else's toes."

"Tell me about a time when you had to assert yourself in a difficult situation?"

- "There was a woman in my last company who began to be curt to not only me but to the other members of the team. I finally asked her if I could speak with her. At first she denied that she had any issues with anyone, but because I listened and didn't judge her, she eventually opened up and told me that she was having personal problems and that she was sorry that she was imposing her problems on the team. She and I became friends, and she began to be relaxed and friendly around the group after that."

- "This is an incident that happened while I was in school. There were some students who would abuse the library as a place to hang out and socialize. It was really annoying some days when the other students including me were trying to study. I took it upon myself to seek out a person who I thought was there the most often. I asked her if I could talk with her in private. She complied. I explained the problem of having to use the library as a quiet place where I could concentrate and that there were other students in the same boat. She listened and said she was having such a good time that she wasn't aware that she and her friends were causing anyone a problem She said they would find a new meeting place, and apparently they did because I never saw her or her friends again."

- "Yes, I actually lost a friend because I had to speak up and be assertive. It was a matter of a man who was coming to work late and leaving early. It wasn't fair to the employees who were coming in on time and working extra, if needed. I talked to our supervisor and explained the problem because I didn't feel it was my place to talk to him directly. The supervisor suggested that the three of us meet. I agreed to attend the meeting. The guy became very angry with me for complaining and as a result never spoke to me again. He did however change his behavior about being late and leaving early."

"Give me an example of a time when you were assertive and took the initiative."

- "At my last company I was promoted to lead person

because of my ability to speak up. I saw a problem and also saw a way to solve the problem. I went to the person in charge to give him my ideas, and he was not only surprised, but he was delighted with the suggestion. I have learned to speak up when I see a more efficient way of doing things."

- "When I saw a need for a new employee orientation program, I spoke to the VP of human resources and was able to initiate a training program for new employees that will allow them to come up to speed on projects much faster than before. I was commended for my idea."

- "I consider myself an assertive person when it comes to internal problems among coworkers. There was an incident among members of our team that was affecting team spirit and our work as well. I spoke directly to the people involved and was able to sit down with them to put the issues on the table. It was a bit touchy for a while. But, because I moderated the discussion and kept everyone in their place, we eventually came to agreement and the misunderstanding was cleared up. Our team was once again functioning as the great team we were."

Negotiations

"Have you been involved in negotiations in your past jobs?"

- "At my last job I was on the 'best practices' team after we merged two companies. Our team went through extensive negotiating to maintain practices that were important to our department. I was the team leader and managed to keep things under control by being as objective as possible."
- "As the HR manager, I was in negotiations with candidates regarding salary offers and benefits on a regular basis. The secret to my successful negotiations was to listen first and then talk."
- "I have strong training in negotiations and was able to negotiate a win/win situation in almost all of the cases I worked on as an arbitrator. Listening and using active listening skills is important when hearing all sides of the problem."

"Tell me about a time when you negotiated a deal at your last job?"

- "The most successful negotiations I have had involved a contract with the shipping dealer who I had to sell over a long period before he agreed to our conditions. But I am happy to report it resulted in a 15 percent reduction in our costs."
- "Negotiating contracts was a major part of the responsibilities at my last job. In fact, I was given a bonus for saving the company over half a million dollars in a six-month period."

- "I was able to negotiate a pretax ROI on a nonregulated gas storage partnership. It was a deal that made me very popular with upper-level managers. In fact, they gave me a promotion based on the deal I was able to put together."

"In your career, what negotiation are you most proud of?"

- "That would be the time I was involved in analyzing and recommending the purchase of a competitor's company. I was instrumental in the research and preparation of an offer that was eventually accepted and that turned out to be a win/win situation for both companies."
- "As an administrative assistant I normally don't get involved in negotiations, but I was the contact with our coffee vendor and had occasion to discuss our problems with some of the products. He wanted our business and said he would make good on any dissatisfaction. I told him that wasn't good enough. He eventually agreed to reduce his fees to keep us as customers. My boss was very impressed that I had taken the initiative and that I was able to negotiate a better deal."
- "As a buyer, my main focus is to evaluate any purchases for the company and to shop around for better deals. I was able to save the company over $10,000 by discovering an outlet that would supply our technical equipment at almost half of what we were paying. The service was satisfactory, and the products were up to our standards. I got a nice bonus for taking the initiative."

Problem Solving

"How would you describe your problem-solving ability?"

- "I have a process that I go through when solving problems —evaluate, explore, research, prepare, and perform. It has helped me through many a tough problem."
- "If you were to ask my last boss, he would tell you that I thrive on problems and coming up with solutions, particularly problems that involve money. I've always been good with numbers and I am very particular about attention to detail."
- "At work they call me, 'Mr. Problem Solver.' I am the one who everyone comes to when no one else can figure out the problem with his or her computer or a system. I like working with people, so I try to make myself available whenever possible."

"Tell me about a time when you solved a problem at work."

- "On one of my past jobs I was able to detect a pattern of events and could see where the problem was occurring. I immediately worked with the engineering department to solve the problem that turned out to be a leak that was causing irregular test results. Working together, we were able to come up with a solution. No one had thought to look for a pattern, and it would have probably gone on for quite a while before anyone had noticed the problem."
- "I recently had an experience where I analyzed some information that had been used for years and found it to be totally inefficient. By presenting a new format and

way of tracking costs, I was able to come up with a way to save significant dollars. Needless to say, the idea was met with much enthusiasm and encouragement. The roll out was a big success."

■ "The problem wasn't big enough for anyone to do anything about. But it was big enough so that everyone was complaining about it every day. It had to do with the scheduling of time so that the mail went out that day. I took it upon myself to draw up a schedule and talk to the delivery guy about the time and pickup. The problem was easily solved, but no one had taken the time to deal with it. I received many pats on the back for taking the initiative."

"Tell me about a time when you solved a difficult problem."

■ "One of my strengths is my analytical problem-solving ability. I had a recent success when I saw that the numbers were down on the sale of our new product. I worked with a cross-functional team and surveyed the customer only to find out that we had been using the wrong approach for our target audience. I made recommendations to the board of directors and after some discussion and tweaking was able to influence them to approve a whole new approach with the customer. The result was a better product launch, more sales, and very satisfied customers."

■ "The toughest problems I have encountered are problems that are the result of an emergency. In my last job I was called in on a Sunday because the power to all the computers in the company had shut down. It was essential that I get in there fast and work on the problem before employees started arriving in the morning. Two technicians

➡

and I worked all day past midnight struggling to get the power back up. We were able to fix the problem so that when employees began arriving on Monday morning, they never knew there had been a significant computer glitch."

- "We had a problem at one of my last jobs with overspending on office supplies. By initiating a process improvement plan, I was able to solve the problem of expensive waste that had been practiced at the company for the previous five years. I was generously rewarded for that solution."

"Tell me about an analytical problem that you solved in your last job."

- "I take an analytical approach and see the project from the viewpoint of the user as well as the provider. I can remember a time when a customer needed some facts before she could decide whether to buy our product. The first thing I did was work with her to find out her needs, and then I was able to analyze what was necessary to make the sale. This is an approach I use consistently when working with customers."

- "I was the key lead in the project when we successfully analyzed the company software for Y2K compliance. Because the team I was working with had done such a thorough job of analyzing the data, we were able to ride through the potential catastrophe with ease. It took a lot of proactive analytical work to pull that project together."

- "When working with groups of people who have different agendas, I have found that standing back and analyzing where each group is coming from helps me understand the situation. I did this with a group I was working with at my last job. By staying objective and detached, I was able to lead the team through a project that resulted in a successful campaign and sales effort."

"Are you required to analyze data at your current job?"

- "Yes, in fact just recently I worked on an interesting study done at the hospital I work for. The project involved tracking patients who were taking a certain drug and then analyzing the data to watch for patterns. My role was to analyze the results and then to enter those results on a spreadsheet that was eventually presented to management. It turned out to be a very successful study."

■ "One of the main functions of my job is analyzing costs and then making recommendations. A recent cost analysis resulted in a major change in the way that costs are tracked. This saved the company more that $1000 a day."

■ "I would say that my job is part analyzing and part customer service. Because the focus has shifted to customer service at the present time, I have had to deal more with the customer one on one. However, analysis is still a major part of my job, and there have been occasions when my analytical skills saved a customer time and money, but it is no longer the main focus of my job."

"What has been your biggest analytical challenge?"

■ "Believe it or not, it was when I did an internship for a Fortune 500 company. The project I worked on was one of the most difficult of my career. I spent long days—as many at 10 to 12 hours data mining. I had a specific project I was working on for human resources and was able to show a correlation between attendance and performance. I presented my findings to the directors and VPs and received great praise for my intense work."

■ "It was while I was working abroad in a marketing department. I could see from the figures I was receiving that there was something wrong with the introduction of a new product. I had the team I worked with go out and interview users to find out why we were missing our mark. It turned out that we were targeting the wrong audience.

➡

My team and I put together a very complete report with facts and figures to support pulling the product and starting over. It was a tough sell to management, but our findings backed our analysis for the change. Managers finally agreed, and the result was very positive."

- "That would be a business development role I had at one of my previous companies. I assumed responsibility for software sales, which entailed collaborating with the implementation team to successfully install document imaging and workflow systems in all 25 locations of the company. After consulting with the team, I developed a cost-benefits and return-on-investment analysis demonstrating the effectiveness of the programs. I gave a presentation to key executives and stakeholders explaining the facts. I won their unanimous approval."

Adaptability

"When have you had to adapt in your work?"

- "My military background has prepared me for this part of any job. When you are on call 24/7, as I was in the Army, you learn quickly to move first, think second. Being flexible and being able to adapt quickly was not only necessary in the service, it was mandatory. I have brought that same skill to my work. I do whatever it takes to get the job done—on time!"

- "In the graphic design and print media business, I have learned that whatever the customer wants is important. This has been a recurring situation working with customers who want last minute changes—and I do mean last minute. I am a very tolerant person who believes in the motto, 'The customer is always right.'"

- "Having had five bosses in three years has been something I've had to adapt to. The problem was that my bosses didn't get to choose me, but they inherited me when they took over the job. As a professional support person I have adapted to my current boss's management and work style. I'm sure if you asked any of my former bosses, they would tell you that I am a professional who knows how to adapt."

"What would you do if you had almost completed a project and the plans changed?"

- "I know this scenario well in the product development area. One particular incident I remember was a project that was within two weeks of completion when the customer called and changed the specs by more than 75 percent. My first thought was, 'Oh, no. This can't be happening,' but then I got a grip and went to work to get the job done according to the customer's requirements. One thing I've learned in this business is to let go and take the projects as they come."

- "I would do what I do best—adapt. I would see what I could salvage from the project that I had been working on and rework it as needed. Then I would make sure that I understood the new requirements. I would want to talk to the customer and find out why the changes were going to make the project better and what I could do to make improvements on the new plans. I would then put my foot to the pedal and move forward."

- "I can't say that this is my favorite part of the job, but it is a part of the job that I have learned to adapt to. 'Change' is the name of the game in this industry. I keep an open mind about change and would do whatever was needed to make the transition as seamless as possible. I haven't had any problem with adapting to change in my career."

"How have you been able to adapt to new situations in the past?"

- "My experience with new situations has been rich because of the layoffs and changes in the computer industry. I was laid off twice because of reductions in force. In fact, one of the companies closed the doors as we walked out. I've had to accept the fact that not all start-up companies are going to make it. I consider myself a risk taker and have been able to quickly transition into new jobs because of my strong programming skills."

- "Since I have been at one company for over 15 years, I haven't had to deal with new situations as such. But I have

71

had to deal with changes as anyone in business has had to. I think the biggest adaptation for me was to go from paper reports to electronic billing. Fortunately, not only do I have a head for figures but for automation as well. I was able to help many others in the company because I was able to pick up the computer skills quickly."

- "Anyone who knows me would tell you that I thrive on change. I live in the now and believe change and adapting to change are a way of life. I have changed jobs and bosses many times in my career with no problems. I have a natural ability to adjust to the situation and the requirements needed to do the job."

Ability to Work with Others

"How would you describe your ability to work with others?"

- "I know that if you were to ask any of my coworkers, they would tell you that one of my strongest traits is my ability to get along with almost everyone. I even get along with people who others consider difficult to work with."

- "Whenever I start at a new company or job, the first thing I do is find out who the people are whom I will need to know in order to get things done. For example, I made friends with the guy in the mailroom within my first two weeks at my last job, and that relationship really paid off. He was a person who knew a lot about what went on in the company and was able to direct me when I needed a resource."

- "I'm not going to say that I get along with everyone because the truth is that at each company where I've worked there have been one or two people who were difficult to get along with. But I will say that I maintain a professional relationship with all the people I work with regardless of their personality or attitude."

"Tell me about a time when you were required to work with people you had not previously worked with."

- "At my previous job our company was acquired, and I was inherited by a group. There seemed to be a natural hostility toward the new guys from the start. I simply went out of my way to make sure that the people in my group knew that I was a team player and that I would help out in anyway I could. Eventually they got the idea that I was on their team and not a threat to them. After a couple of months I was friends with almost everyone on the team."

■ "That was when I was in college and had to work with a team for a project management class. At first it seemed that we were each pulling in different directions, but then alliances started forming. What I found worked for me in this situation was to show an interest in the other person's interest. It's amazing how easy it is to make friends when you are willing to listen and put yourself second."

■ "In the military you become 'soul brothers and sisters' with everyone very fast. It's a matter of relying on one another. I made fast friends with a woman who came into the group when I did. We were both newcomers and didn't feel welcome at first. We kept a low profile and offered suggestions only when we felt it was appropriate or would save time. She and I continued to be friends the whole time I was stationed at that location, but we both branched out to make other friends as the weeks passed."

"What are the biggest challenges you face when you are required to work with others?"

■ "I consider myself a low-key person when it comes to socializing. I can deal with anyone when it is about work, but when it comes to socializing, I tend to pull back until I know the people I'm with better. In this job I want to have a more active role in some of the fund-raising and other events that interest me."

■ "The biggest challenge for me is getting to know the personality type of each person I'm dealing with so that I can determine what communication style he or she prefers. By listening and observing I can pretty much figure out the preference of most people. I then try to accommodate that person's needs by adjusting my vocabulary to fit his or her style."

- "I don't see it as a challenge but more of a process I go through in getting to know people and what their role is within the company. I am very observant of other's behavior, and I watch them in action before I judge. This is actually the part of the job that I like best."

Meeting Deadlines

"Tell me about a time you had to meet multiple deadlines in a short period. How were you able to accomplish this?"

- "I can remember one particularly hectic holiday period when there were orders stacked knee deep. There was one woman who kept calling and wanting to know when her package would arrive. I was working on her details when I received another call telling me that the CFO had to be picked up from the airport and driven to her house. The first thing I did was to ask the woman if I could possibly call her in the morning. Because I had been so polite with her from the beginning, she actually agreed to wait. I was then able to focus and on the task of picking up the CFO at the airport."

- "I'm one of those people who thrives on deadlines. It's exciting to see how much people can accomplish when they are under time pressure. I was able to get my crew to work overtime and weekends to send out several crucial orders that were on the same deadline. They did it and of course I rewarded them for their efforts."

- "I have worked with some fantastic teams during my career. There was one time at the company before my last job where a team pulled together to get a project completed that had multiple layers. I simply divided up the different tasks and we worked like one big machine. We not only completed the project, but we came in before the deadline. I really enjoy good teamwork."

"Tell me about a time you were unable to meet an important deadline. How did you handle this?"

- "There was one job I had where I was unable to satisfy the customer's request. I had done everything in my power to pull it off, but I had to call and talk to the customer and convince him that I needed two or three more days before I could complete his job. He wasn't happy, but when I told him about the quality that I was striving for, he allowed me three extra days. As it turned out, I only needed a day and a half before I was able to complete the project and send it to the customer."

- "I have never really been unable to meet a deadline, but there was one time in my career when I almost broke my record. The upgrades had not arrived for me to complete the installation of parts in a machine. Even though I had placed numerous calls to try to expedite the shipment, they weren't going to make the deadline. I got on the phone and called every local supplier that I could find. I was able to find a small shop that said that if I were willing to drive across town, they would have the parts ready for me. I did, and I was able to meet my deadline and hold my record of never missing a deadline."

- "This is an unfortunate story that I prefer not to tell, but since you asked, I will tell you about an order that did not get shipped and cost the company several thousands of dollars. I hadn't verified shipment of an order, which I normally did, and it was late getting to us and in turn we didn't get it to the customers when they needed it. The order was cancelled, and the revenue lost. I learned a valuable lesson about follow-through from that experience."

"Deadlines are an important part of this job. How do you feel about this?"

- "I think deadlines are the most important part of any support person's job. If I don't meet my deadline, it will affect everyone up the chain of command. I am very conscientious about deadlines."

- "Two things I pride myself on are my ability to meet deadlines and my punctuality. Both require some forethought and planning. If at all possible I will get whatever project I am working on in by the deadline."

- "I consider myself a responsible, hard worker. Part of getting any job done is meeting obligations expected of you on time. Whether it's getting to work on time or getting information and following up with a customer, I always will do everything I can to observe time demands and deadlines."

Decisiveness

"Tell me about a time when you were required to make a decision that could have had potential negative outcomes. How did you make this decision?"

- "I had to decide what members of the team we could do without. They were to be laid off as a result of my decision. I struggled with the names, but in the end I chose the stronger members of the team to stay."

- "Part of leading a team is making decisions that could have an impact on the outcome of a project. I knew that the costs of a certain project we were working on were going to exceed budget, but I made the decision to move forward anyway. In the end the project was completed, but the rewards promised were not fulfilled. It was a negative experience that I have tried to avoid in all my jobs since that one."

- "I had to make a decision whether to give information to my boss that would change the nature of our project before we even got started. I could have held the information back, and we would have all had several months' work. But in the end I had to share my information with the head of the department. The information had a negative effect on the morale of the group for some time. I feel I did the right thing even though it was a tough decision at the time."

"You may be required to make key decisions when I'm out of the office. How do you feel about that?"

- "I was acting supervisor at my last position a great deal of the time. I had to make decisions about money expenditures and discipline of staff. I think decision-making comes with the territory of more responsibility. I know I have what it takes to use sound judgment when it comes to decisions."

■ "This was exactly the case in my last job. I was left in charge while my boss did project consulting. I had to learn how to make decisions to survive in that job. I have done the job for more than two years now and feel it has been a great training ground for this job. Decisions are often a matter of knowing whom to consult before taking action."

■ "Since an early age, I have had a good head on my shoulders for making decisions. I showed that I could be trusted in my last company. Even though I don't want to stay there anymore, I know I have been highly thought of because of my sound judgment."

"Have you ever made the wrong decision about a project?"

■ "I wish I could say that I never made a wrong decision, but I would be lying. I have had to make quick decisions on many projects and have made some without the proper information. In one case it did delay the shipment of an important order, and that subsequently cost the company extra dollars. I can tell you that every time I've ever made a mistake I've also learned a valuable lesson. I have had enough experience to know how to avoid most of the mistakes involved in this line of work."

■ "Unfortunately, I made some wrong decisions on predicting investments, especially in the early years of my career. I did not allow for the unexpected and got caught short more than once. Through experience in dealing with the

➡

investment market, I have learned to calculate the risk and to factor in the unexpected. I have a formula that I always keep in mind when making decisions. It came from a sign in my Dad's workshop:'Measure twice, cut once.' That saying has kept me from making hasty decisions more than once."

- "The only way to learn is to make mistakes. I make mistakes from time to time, but I have never made a mistake that jeopardized my reputation or that of the company. Sometimes the orders get mixed up or the prices are misquoted, but overall I have an excellent record. My teammates would tell you that I am fastidious when it comes to attention to detail."

Initiative

"Give me an example of a recent incident where you took the initiative on a project."

- "We were having a problem with our ordering procedure with one particular customer. I went to the Web site and researched it frame-by-frame until I found the problem. I presented the problem to our technical department, and we worked out the problem together. I then went to the customers and trained them on the use of the system. I sat with them and went through the procedure step by step until they were able to get the hang of it. Afterward I continued to follow up until I knew the problem was resolved."

- "I volunteer as an assistant coach of a basketball team for youths at risk. I observed that the stronger players were playing more than the other players but that they were not necessarily winning. I also observed that the mediocre players had some talent in other ways, like shooting and defending, and they weren't being used. I thought that if we could mix the strengths of all of the players, we would have a stronger chance of winning. I took the idea to the head coach, and he gave me the go-ahead. I held a team meeting and explained my idea that was met with some resistance but was eventually accepted on a trial basis. We practiced and practiced and then began winning games. We ranked second that year, but if I hadn't taken the initiative, we would have ranked in the teens. But more than winning, in the end the players had a real sense of 'team.'"

- "One successful idea I initiated was a way of encouraging people to pay their payments on time during the holidays. I suggested rewarding people who sent on-time payments by contributing a portion of their payments to their favorite charity. Because it was the holiday season, people were more into helping others. Senior managers agreed to the idea because they could write off the contribution. It was implemented with an announcement to card holders and met with a surprising 10 percent increase in on-time payments. Everybody won on that venture."

"When I say the word 'initiative,' what is the first thought that comes into your mind."

- "The first thought that I have is 'stepping up to the plate.' As both a team player and a sports fan I can relate to the concept of taking a turn at bat. I have stepped up to the bat and even hit a few 'home runs' with successful ideas during my five years as a marketing analyst."
- "'Action' is the first word that comes to mind. In order to take the initiative, you have to be willing to take a risk, and that usually involves doing something. I am the type of person who is a 'doer.' It's one thing to have an idea, but a company has to have an equal number of 'doers' in order to get the job done."
- "I think of 'above and beyond.' Not just doing what is expected but taking whatever actions are necessary to get the job done, and done right. If you were to ask my boss, he would tell you that he is always pleased with my ability to take the initiative and to follow through until the action is completed."

"Would you still take the initiative on a project if you knew you weren't going to be recognized for it?"

- "My rewards are fulfilling my values. One of my top values is job satisfaction and part of satisfaction is doing the job right, whether I'm recognized for it or not."

- "I'm afraid that the type of work that I do is seldom recognized, but I'm expected to perform at the highest level. Because I have such a high work ethic, it is important for me to please myself. I am not saying that I don't mind a pat on the back now and then. I have just learned not to expect them."
- "My self-motivation serves as a reward. I have received many awards for work I have done, and that has been great. But the real rewards are from my knowing that I made a difference in the work or in the fact that I made someone else's life or job easier."

Flexibility

"This job requires a lot of flexibility. How do you do in this type of environment?"

- "I believe 'change' is the name of the game these days. In my last job I had seven different bosses in five years. Because I am self-disciplined and motivated, I have been able to adjust my style to the needs of each boss I have had—and done it with success."

- "Anyone who doesn't realize that the 'job' as we have known it in the past has changed has been living under a rock. I welcome variety and change, and I work hard in whatever environment I am placed. I consider myself a very adaptable and flexible person."

- "I happen to thrive on change and variety. No matter what company I have worked for or what position I have held, I have been able to adapt quickly to change. I have worked for three companies that have gone through mergers or acquisitions, and I was very successful in adapting to the new environments without any problem."

"How comfortable are you with change?"

- "I am comfortable with the changing of procedures, especially when it is communicated in a factual way. If I can see the rationale for the change, then it is easier for me to accept. If I don't understand the change, I will speak up with questions so that I can understand how the change affects me or my work."

- "Experience has been the best teacher for me in accepting change. I have gone through many changes in the start-up company I worked for last. Change is really the nature of a start-up, and if I hadn't accepted that fact, I wouldn't have survived there for over four years. Overall, it was an exciting experience because of all the changes."

- "I grew up in a military family, and change is a way of life that I know well. I attended five schools before I graduated from high school. It was challenging at times, but I learned to adapt and make friends quickly. That trait has served me well in this fast-paced work environment."

"Our clients frequently ask for projects to be changed mid-process. Tell me how you've dealt with similar clients in the past."

- "In the printing and publishing business that is an every-day occurrence. There was one woman I worked with who made changes right up until the time we went to press. I eventually began to call her every time we were set to go to make sure that we weren't going to have to do it over because she changed her mind. She told me how much I helped her by accepting her behavior and working with her instead of getting frustrated and angry."

- "There have been many late nights working in a legal office. Sometimes it seems as though everything is a 'red hot' action item. One time I stayed working with a team of attorneys and paralegals until 2:00 A.M. to assist in the preparation of a brief that had to be done for the next day's court session. I have to admit that we fed off each other's energy, and the team spirit was high. This enabled us to finish in a timely manner. The main thing was that we accomplished the task before the deadline."

- "There was an incident with a product that was ready to be shipped out when the customer called and wanted a change made before it shipped. This action required my team and me to work over the weekend to accommodate the change. The company I worked for was a firm believer, as am I, that the customer is always right. We put in the overtime and shipped the product according to the customer's requirements."

Organizational Skills

"Describe your organizational skills."

- "The first thing I do in the morning is check my list of things I want to accomplish that day. I then prioritize them according to urgency. I allow time for the unexpected, and if all goes according to plan and I don't use the extra time, then I have time for the proactive things I like to do. Most days my plan can be followed about 80 percent of the time, but there are days when only 30 percent of the plan gets done. I just prefer to have a plan."

- "I really like technical toys. I have a Palm Pilot and a laptop that serve me well in organizing my day as well as my life. Once in a while I even carry around a 'to do list' as another means of keeping me on track. If the day doesn't go according to the plan, then I reprioritize and do what didn't get done on the following day if possible. I have learned that flexibility is essential to being well organized. I have learned to roll with the punches so to speak."

- "I have been responsible for planning many events that I couldn't have possibly done without being organized. I use a word processing system and Excel spreadsheets to plan my projects and to track the progress day to day. One of my strongest skills is being organized and using the tools necessary to be that way."

"How well do you work with unorganized people?"

- "One of my favorite sayings is that 'I can bring order to chaos,' and I have done just that. I have worked for many bosses who were very disorganized. Once I started showing them how they could track their activities on software, they began to change the way they were doing things. My last boss shared his schedule with me each day, and I was able to jump in when needed. He really praised me for helping him improve his organizational skills."

- "Everybody has his or her own way of working. I am very organized in my work life and have a very organized filing system. Others are more interested in results than they are the details of keeping track. I have been a very valued support person because of my keen organizational ability and my ability to keep the work grounded when there is a problem."

- "One of my strengths is working with all kinds of people. I simply adjust my style to meet their needs. Whether it's planning or doing, I offer my strengths in a way that is very nonthreatening to the people I am working with. I would never want people to feel that I am judging their work because they do not have the same way of organizing that I have. I like to help, not judge."

"Your résumé states that you are organized. How would you describe your organizational style?"

- "My coworkers would tell you that they call me 'Ms. Organized,' because I always have a schedule and a plan. I have to admit that I prefer to plan and not be rushed. I can also adapt quickly and change my plans if I have to, but I like to start out with a plan to begin the day."

- "I have a very organized system that I can access any information that I require to do my job. I've always been a very organized and detail-oriented person. My bosses have rewarded me when my skills have saved them from making the wrong decision because of a lack of information. All they have to do is ask, and I can provide what they need. I take great pleasure in doing that."

- "I would describe my organizational skills as excellent. My key strength is my ability to organize and coordinate projects or events. I get great satisfaction when I can bring order to a space or to a situation."

Ability to Learn on the Job

"You'll be required to hit the ground running for this job. How will you be able to handle this?"

- "From what you've been telling me about the requirements of the job, I will have no trouble hitting the ground running. The first thing I do at any job is read whatever information there is about the position or department. Once I have the procedures outlined, I begin to make contacts to locate resources within the working situation. In every job I've held, I have been up and running in a matter of a week or so."

- "This job is very similar to the job that I performed at the bank I worked for. I am sure that the forms are different and maybe some of the procedures, but I am very well trained in handling deposits and customers. I would feel confident that with some time to collect information and observe I would be ready to try my own wings within a matter of days."

- "I pride myself as being one of the fastest people I know to come up to speed on a new job. I will stay and learn whatever I have to by reading and talking to others so that I can move into the position as soon as possible. I've managed this technique in my previous three jobs, and every boss I've had was surprised at my ability to pick up information so quickly."

"How did you go about learning a new skill when it was required for the job?"

- "In my last job, the learning was by trial and error. There was very little training provided and no time to spend training me on the details. I just jumped in, and when I ran into a barrier, I would try to resource the answer either by reading or by conferring with a coworker. If that method didn't work, as a last resort I would take the problem to my supervisor. It didn't take me long before people were coming to me with questions."

■ "I am a voracious reader. I read anything and everything. Before I even started my last job, I learned about new trends in the industry and the systems that were being used. When I got on the job, I read through every manual and instruction sheet that I could get my hands on. In a very short time I was as knowledgeable as some of the employees that had been with the company for several years. I was sensitive not to make anyone feel that I had outrun him or her in such a short time. I consider myself a person who works well within a team environment."

■ "Because I had taken classes in accounting in college, I had a basic understanding of the fundamentals of finance. When I was given a ledger to work with, I quickly accessed information from the Internet that refreshed what I needed to know. I find the Internet to be the equivalent of having millions of resources at my fingertips. I was up to speed in no time by reviewing the information I had learned in school."

"Tell me about the most recent skill you acquired on the job. How did you acquire this skill?"

■ "When we converted from paper to electronic files, the whole department had to learn the new way of filing. I was sent to the corporate office in another state and spent a week there learning the system. I have a natural

92

ability for working with numbers, and I do well with technology. After the training I was able to come back and step into the job with ease. In fact, people would come to me for assistance."

- "I find that most systems are basically the same with a lot of detail to remember. I had to attend classes to learn my current job's data entry system. I learn very quickly, so I took copious notes and really listened to the details of what was being said. Immediately after the class I went back to the office and began to do trial entries before any of the details faded. My notes and my quick learning style allowed me to learn the system so easily that I was able to train my coworkers who started when I did."

- "I recently learned online teaching techniques by taking an online class. It was an interesting experience to go through the assignments and to communicate and partner with people in a virtual manner. I found the techniques of communicating through message boards and discussing views with one another to be very effective. The best part of this approach to learning is that you can do it at your own convenience."

Prioritizing

"What is your process for setting priorities?"

■ "I am a multitasker and have no problem with several projects going on at the same time. I am constantly prioritizing and adjusting projects to make sure that the most urgent projects are dealt with first. I also have established a reputation as a person who knows how to get things done, so I can negotiate a deadline if needed and the other person will feel confident that I will honor my commitment."

■ "When I worked as a support person for the sales team, this was one of my biggest challenges, keeping everyone satisfied or at least not dissatisfied. I start the day with a list of the tasks I have to accomplish and put them in the order of how each might affect service. If a customer has a problem, I try to deal with that as quickly as possible. I am very customer–service-oriented and always make sure the customer comes first. I also consider the internal needs such as executives or managers who need their priorities dealt with. I have worked with great teams, and we have been there for one another when priorities collided."

■ "I actually like working in a fast-paced environment where there is a need to prioritize and juggle projects. I usually work with the hottest buttons first and then set a schedule to meet required deadlines. Some of the more 'back burner' projects get worked in as time allows. But I review those projects on a weekly basis so they don't get forgotten. Overall I would rate myself high as a person who can do many things at the same time and still meet deadlines."

"What would you do if your priorities conflict with the priorities of someone you work with on a project?"

- "I consider customers in two categories; external customers and internal customers. When I am working with or for someone on a project and there is a conflict, I take into consideration his or her needs as an internal customer. I have had great success at negotiating timelines and also with delegating to others when pushed to the max. When all else fails, I do whatever it takes to get the job done and will stay late or work on a weekend to meet my customer's needs whether it's internal or external."

- "The secret to working with anyone on a project is open communications. Although some people are easier to work with than others, I always try to get whatever the issues are on the table so that we can discuss them. I have found that by talking out the conflicts and priorities rationally we have been able to come up with mutually agreeable solutions."

- "My style as a team player has allowed me to have a little slack when it comes to working with others. Because my team members know that I have a high work ethic and that my word is as good as done, they have trusted me when I ask for extra time or have to negotiate some help to meet a deadline."

"What has been your biggest challenge in setting priorities?"

- "My biggest challenge is to try to please everyone. Of course, it is impossible to please everyone, but my experience with supporting groups is that each person thinks his or her work should come first. I try to be reasonable and try to treat everyone as equal no matter what working style I run up against. Working with groups has taught me whom I can ask to give me some extra time and whom I need to move quickly for before he or she explodes."

- "I would say that coping with the unexpected has been the biggest challenge. I plan my day and set my priorities, and then all of a sudden there is an emergency and my plans go out the window. I consider myself to be flexible and adapt quickly to new situations, but some days it is a challenge, and I have had to push through the barriers to succeed at my tasks. The good news is that I have been able to do it with an inner energy that exists deep inside me when I have to respond to whatever the situation calls for."

- "I have worked with every type of boss you can imagine, and every one of them would tell you that I have the ability to rise to whatever challenge is thrown at me. I am a calm person most of the time, but when things get really crazy, I actually get more centered and let the rest of the office whirl around me. Some people refer to me as the 'anchor.'"

"How do you approach long-term projects?"

- "Fortunately I was taught early in my education how to outline a project and segment it into parts. This has worked extremely well for me in planning out longer-term projects. I allow myself extra time because I know that the unexpected is sure to be a factor in my plan. I almost always have long-term projects finished weeks before the due date so that I have time to review and rethink the details before I submit them."

- "Because I work well under pressure, I sometimes don't give long-term projects the time that I could. But I get a certain rush from the pressure to succeed. I have never missed a deadline—long term or short term. I am very 'in the moment' when I work. One method that works well for me is to keep a binder for each new project and add ideas whenever I get them. I find this to be very helpful when I do sit down to put it all together. I just piece the ideas together and work full speed ahead."

- "I use software spreadsheets to manage my long-term projects. I break the project into equal segments and then check off the tasks as I move through the schedule. This has been very effective in coordinating projects with others as well."

"How would you describe your ability to manage your time?"

- "I was always taught that 'time is money' and to value time as such. I plan my day so that I know how much time each task will require. If something gets cancelled, I use that time to do my long-term projects. If something gets added, I move my priorities around so that I can get the things that I have to do that day done on time and move the less urgent things to tomorrow's schedule."

- "I consider my time management skills to be my strongest asset. For as long as I can remember, I have always organized my work every day and plan in reverse to meet my appointments and deadlines. In other words, if I have to be somewhere at 2:00 P.M., I start planning when I will have to leave for that appointment hours before I actually leave. If you asked people who know me, they would tell you I am very reliable when it comes to being on time."

- "When it comes to time management, I am very dependable. In fact as a support person I had to remind my boss when she had to be somewhere and how long it would take her to get there. My last boss was a last-minute person who would have missed many airplanes if I hadn't reminded her to leave hours before the flight. She considered me her 'right-hand man.'"

"If two people give you projects to be completed by the end of the day and you only have time to do one, how do you proceed?"

- "This goes hand in hand with prioritizing. I would look at the deadline and the importance of the impact of that deadline and then make a decision. I will always ask first if there is any leeway in deadlines. If there isn't, I would try to get help or push until I got it done. I have had to work with people when it was impossible to do the two things at once and have found that if I am willing to push and do whatever I can, they have been willing to let go a bit as well."

- "Sometimes I just have to admit that I will do whatever I can but that one of the projects may be late. I find that attitude makes a huge difference when there is a clash in priorities. I am known for my cooperative spirit, and most people will understand that I can do only so much. I have never had a time when I couldn't work out some kind of a compromise."

- "I have had to arrange a conference call with the two people to discuss the priority of the projects. By putting it out on the table and letting them both know the situation, I have found people to be somewhat reasonable in giving and taking. I think the important thing is to talk this type of problem through rather than trying and failing. No one wins in that situation, and everyone is disappointed. I am big believer in open communications to solve problems."

Chapter Four

The Difficult Questions

This chapter deals with questions that are sensitive and can be uncomfortable to answer. Many of these questions may have a negative undertone and seem to be asking, "Tell us something that is wrong with you." The interviewer is looking to see if past problems are going to follow you to this job. Many of the questions ask for examples of your past behavior—"behavioral questions." You will notice in the example answers that part of the perfect phrase you use takes the focus off of the negative factors and instead accentuates the positive qualities that you bring to the job.

By thinking about and preparing for this type of question before the interview, you will feel more confident about the circumstances of negative situations. You will be able to look the interviewer in the eye as you answer with confidence, talking about those times that you would just as soon forget.

Dealing with Conflict

"Tell me about a time when you had a conflict in your work and how you resolved it."

■ "I usually get along very well with everyone, but there was an incident with a person who was not pulling his weight on the team and all the members of the team were getting disgruntled. I took it upon myself to have a talk with the person when the opportunity presented itself. He was defensive at first but eventually confided in me that he had some family problems at home that were affecting his energy and patience. Once we talked, he made a special effort to be more receptive. The key to resolving this was letting him know that I wasn't judging; just caring."

■ "A woman at my last job was known to be very difficult to get along with. I figured that this was her problem, and I worked with her as a professional. I gave her the respect I would give any coworker when we work together. She seemed to appreciate that I was treating her as a professional, and as a result we were able to work well together."

■ "I volunteer as a basketball coach for disadvantaged kids in my spare time. Last season I had a team that didn't seem to understand the concept of team. I decided that rather than preach at them I would take them out for some fun and bonding. We all went out for pizza one evening and sat around and got to know one another. They seemed to let down their guards when they were away from the court. We ate a lot of pizza that season, but it really made a difference to get them off the court. We became a stronger team and even placed in the finals for the season."

"Have you ever had a conflict at work that you couldn't resolve? What did you do?"

- "It was when I was new at an accounting job. There was a woman there who had been there for four years, and I expected her to take the lead. We had a problem communicating because of a difference in expectations from each other. I approached her and tried to talk to her to see if we could find some common ground. Unfortunately it did not work out. My boss got involved to see what he could do and set the two of us down to see if we could work things out. We just had different personalities and work standards, and we finally agreed to disagree but to treat each other with respect as professionals. We continued to work together on projects, but as professionals and not friends."

- "When I was a volunteer working with a group of scouts, I had an encounter with a parent that didn't get resolved but eventually became a moot issue. One parent did not agree with the way I was organizing things and was very vocal about it. I tried to tell him that all the decisions I make are in the best interest of the troop. But he thought my ideas were holding his child back. We had several exchanges that didn't result in agreement. Eventually his child moved on and graduated to a new level in the program. I felt that I had reason to hold to my position and protect the whole group."

- "I was a student when this happened. I was assigned to work on a group project with five other members of the class. We all met, and each person took a share of the work. After meeting a second time it became apparent that one guy was not participating or doing his part of the project. It began to be a big problem and was affecting team morale. I talked to him one day and found out that he was flunking another class. He ended up withdrawing from the class and program. I felt bad that I couldn't help, but apparently he had just taken on too much. The rest of us had to pull together and complete the project without him, but we managed and received a good grade for our efforts."

"How do you deal with conflicts you have with customers?"

- "I truly believe that 'the customer is always right.' Sometimes I have to bite my tongue and hold back what I would like to say, but I have never insulted a client. I always keep in mind that I represent the company and any action or words that I use reflect on the company—good and bad."

- "When it comes to clients, I know that they are my main customer and that they pay the bills. It is sometimes difficult when the customer is very demanding, but I always try to hear what the problem is and to let the customer know that I heard. If I can't accommodate the request, I try to communicate in as professional manner as possible."

- "One skill that I am very proud of is my patience. This is the skill that sets me apart from my colleagues when it comes to customer service. It sometimes takes great patience to listen and explain the policy or procedure to the customer. I always treat people the way I want to be treated even when they are nasty to me. I try to put myself in their shoes and address the issue from that point of view as often as I can."

"Tell me about a time when you had to react quickly to a situation."

- "We often have rush orders, which means that we have to drop everything and run. We had a situation like that last month where the customer wanted a delivery in the evening mail. Fortunately, I know a post office that is open until midnight. I had to work until almost that time to meet this deadline, but I was able to do it. I am known for doing whatever it takes to get the job done."

- "When I was an officer in the military, I had a crew of eight men under me. We were on our way home to a much-needed leave when we received orders to return to the country we had just left. There was a national emergency at the time, and we had no recourse. I had to do some sympathetic talking to try to get morale back up, pointing out that we were doing something that was going to make a difference. Outside we all accepted the assignment and did our job. Inside we were all really feeling down. In the end we did the job we signed on to do."

- "On my way out of the office one night I received a 'panic' call from a key customer. He needed a document sent to him by 8:00 A.M. the next day. There was nothing to do but to back track and start my day over instead of ending it. I worked two extra hours and then drove to a post office to send the document by next day express. I got the job done. The customer was grateful, and that's what matters to me."

"Many of our clients are frequently in crisis mode. How would you work in such an environment?"

- "You might say that I am the 'calm' in the eye of the storm. I have a unique ability to stay level-headed when things get out of control. I find that talking less and listening more is the answer to handling clients in crisis."

- "Have you ever heard of the term 'whirling dervishes'? When customers are whirling, I stay centered and let them whirl around me. When I see that they're running out of steam, I step in and talk in a very calm and quiet voice. I ask questions to make sure that I understand the problem and then deal with the problem. You'd be surprised at how effective this is."

- "When I took my last job, I was able to prove very early in the game that I was the person who could handle escalated problems. First of all I use a voice that shows confidence and authority, and I let the customer know that I am there for him or her. Second, I am very analytical about solving problems, and I make sure that I explore as many options for solution as possible. Last, I make sure that the customer knows that I will do whatever I can to get him or her through this crisis."

"Have you ever had a crisis you couldn't deal with?"

- "We had a fire in our office, and, as you can imagine, it was very scary as smoke began to fill the rooms. I kept calm throughout the ordeal and attempted to get some of the important ledgers and disks to take with me, but the smoke became too thick too fast. I had to leave with everyone else. I felt I had failed in retrieving valuable information, but everything happened so fast that life became more important than documents."

- "I don't know that this would qualify as a crisis, but it was a big deal for me. In my first job I inadvertently sent out the wrong project information to the wrong customer. It was big because there was proprietary information included. I quickly contacted the delivery service as soon as I realized the mistake, and I was able to retrieve one of the two packages before it was opened. The other package unfortunately was opened, and I had to take the responsibility for my mistake. I can tell you that I never made that error again."

- "I can't remember a real crisis, but I have had some unpleasant moments when I've made mistakes. One time I forgot to include some expensive software in a pricing calculation, and the company had to stand behind my quote even though it took a loss. That particular day it felt like the biggest crisis of my career. I learned a valuable lesson about taking my time and checking my figures twice before making commitments."

"Give me an example of a time when you weren't able to deal successfully with a problem."

- "We were having a problem meeting a deadline at my last job. My boss told us that for each day over the deadline, there would be money subtracted from the bonus we were promised. You can imagine how that news went over. But there is nothing like money to motivate a team of workers. I came up with the idea of cross-functional teams to complete our task. Each person paired up with a person who did a different job. By working in tandem, we were able to do twice the steps in half the time. It was a bit confusing for the first couple of days, but it really boosted morale. Everybody was pulling toward a common goal. We came in two days late, but it could have been much worse. In the end we all laughed about working so hard and getting penalized for our efforts. It was the most stressful and fun time I've ever had on a job."

- "This is one of those stories without a happy ending. I usually have a planned schedule for every step of a project. There was a time however when my plan was not as well thought out as usual, and it started to fall apart. I hadn't allowed extra time for problems or emergencies. I had cut it too close to begin with, and of course this is the time my computer chose to crash. It was chaotic for a while until I called and located a computer that wasn't being used for a few days. I was able to retrieve most of my data, and I did complete the job. Unfortunately, my best efforts and resourcefulness didn't kick in quick enough, so I missed the deadline, but I learned a valuable lesson in the process. That hasn't happened to me again."

- "There was one incident when I couldn't deal with a problem in the office, and I was sorry after that I hadn't. We had a customer who was taking advantage of the situation by using our service as a means to get free technical assistance, even when it was not our product she needed help with. I helped her because she was a good customer, and I saw others doing the same thing for this customer. Eventually it was reported that this woman was abusing the services, and she quit the service. I always regretted not taking the initiative and speaking directly to her. I learned a lesson from that incident which has helped me handle similar problems in a more assertive manner."

Past Career Baggage

"I noticed from your résumé that you left your last job after only a year. Was there a specific reason?"

- ■ "Unfortunately, the company I was working for was going through some tough economic times and had a series of layoffs. I survived three rounds, but the last one got me. My whole department was laid off. I really liked the work I was doing there and hope to find a similar job with some of the same type of responsibilities. I applied for this job because it looks like a perfect match for me and the skills that I can bring to the job."

- ■ "My record over the last four years has been excellent, and I would be glad to give any of my bosses as a reference. Unfortunately, I have to admit that I was fired from my last job because of poor judgment. It was a joke that went too far. I'm sorry that it happened and can tell you that I learned a very costly lesson as a result. I can assure you that I won't make that mistake, or one like it, again. I'm ready to start with a clean slate and focus on my strengths as a loyal manager and the value of my experience that I can bring to this company."

- ■ "As a senior manager I was responsible for the people who reported to me. One of my managers made a very serious banking error that should never have happened. But it did. He was called on the carpet for it and was fired. Because I was his manager, I too was fired. I take responsibility for the mistake because it happened on 'my watch.' I will always stand behind any of the people who work with me regardless of what happens. We both learned a difficult

➥

lesson and had to pay the price. I know I have the skills and adaptability to avoid such mistakes in the future."

"It looks like you've jumped from job to job for the past five years. Can you explain that?"

- "The job market's instability has kept me jumping. I was laid off for the first time five years ago and was able to get a new position very quickly. Unfortunately the company I went to work for was acquired, and I was laid off again after two years. My last job took longer to obtain because of the great number of people competing for the same jobs. When I finally did get the position I wanted, the company relocated to another state. I'm afraid I have been in the wrong place at the wrong time. I am now looking for a 'home' in my next job with the intention of settling in for a longer duration."

- "If you look closely at my résumé you will see that I've actually been at the same job for the past seven years. It's the company that has changed. The company I originally went to work for was HSF, which merged with another company and became HFP after I was there two years. Then in 2000 HFP was acquired by DWE, and my position was changed. So, actually I have worked in the same building, doing the same work while taking on added responsibility. It's just on paper that I've moved around so much."

- "Yes, unfortunately the last two companies that I worked for have moved some functions to corporate headquarters in other states to consolidate costs. In both cases I was asked to transfer, but for family reasons I have chosen to stay in this area."

"I see from your résumé that you have an 18-month period where you didn't work. What was going on during that time?"

- "I did take time off for personal reasons. I was fortunate that I was able to take a sabbatical from my work. I am now ready to resume my career with a new excitement and energy to give my new job."

- "When I was laid off from my last job, my wife and I made a decision to make an investment in our long-term future. I decided it was in my interest to pursue my MBA. I entered an 18-month program as a full-time student and didn't work during that time. This additional education allows me to view business from a broader perspective and to move more ably toward my career goals."

- "After being laid off twice, I decided to take a time-out from the workplace and to pursue some other interests and deal with some family obligations. For six months I did not seek employment at all. After the beginning of the year I began a very selective search. I have to admit it has taken longer than I had expected, but I would rather find the right company with a viable career path than to jump at the first offer I receive."

Getting Fired

"Have you ever been fired from a position?"

- "Yes, I was fired early in my work career. I can't remember all the details since it was several years back, but I can still remember the horrible feeling attached to being fired. I changed my work ethic and attitude after that experience and have never come close to being fired again."

- "I was fired from the job before my last job. While I don't want to place blame, my boss was known for being demanding and difficult to work for. I lasted longer than any of his other assistants. But one day I made a mistake, and he blew up and fired me. I really should have left before that time, but the economy was tight and I was glad to have a job. It was a bad situation from the beginning."

- "I was fired because of a disagreement between a coworker and me. We were both fired for unprofessional conduct. I think it was a fair call to let us both go rather than to take sides. We were both in the wrong. I learned from that. When there is a disagreement now, I go out of my way to avoid it or go through proper channels to resolve the conflict. It was a difficult way to learn that lesson."

"I know you were fired from your previous job. Can you explain the circumstances?"

- "Being fired is like having a black mark on my record. I am very disappointed in myself, and I can assure you that I would handle the situation differently if I could go back and do it again. It was about a joke that went too far, and there was a claim of sexual harassment by a woman. I am

112

sorry that I was a part of the joke, and I apologized to everyone involved. But I had to accept the consequences of my actions."

- "I wasn't exactly fired, but I was asked to leave. I could blame it on my boss, but that would be unprofessional. Suffice it to say that my boss and I were very different in the way we saw things. Although we operated on a very professional basis at all times, it was agreed that I should move on. It was a very good move, and I regret not doing it earlier."

- "The circumstances around my being fired are still some-what vague, even to me. When the company went through a major reorganization, I got a new boss. She had worked in another department with a support person she had worked with for many years. She wanted that support person with her, and that made me dispensable. If you check the references, they might say I was fired for performance reasons, but the boss I had before that one gave me only the highest performance ratings. It was better to move on than to not be wanted."

"You were recently laid off. How has this affected you?"

- "Being laid off after so many years of loyalty is not easy. I really loved my job and the company and didn't feel good about leaving, but I am mature enough to know that these things happen and I have to move forward. Hopefully I will find a similar job where I can be a loyal employee and key contributor."

- "I have to admit that being laid off after seven months with the company came as a shock. I guess it was a case of being in the wrong job at the wrong time. I'd done my homework and had researched the company before I accepted the offer, but the company being acquired by another company was something I hadn't foreseen."

■ "I consider myself lucky to have survived eight previous rounds of layoffs. The company has been going through a difficult time for the last few years, and it is doing whatever it can to keep afloat. I guess bracing myself every time I heard that there was going to be another layoff prepared me for 'my turn.' There is almost a feeling of relief that I am moving forward to new opportunities ahead."

Working for a Problem Company

"I noticed on your application that you have been working with a company that has been in the news lately. Can you tell me about that?"

- "Yes, the company has taken some hits since the news about the CEO being in trouble. I can tell you it sure made a difference in my stock investments. As far as my work in the company goes, I did my job as a marketing person and was not affected in any way by the problem. It's still a good company. It's just time for me to move in another direction."

- "It's been a challenge for me to have that company name on my résumé right now. If I had been involved in some of the decisions made, I might feel responsible, but the truth is that I was hit as hard if not harder than anyone who had invested in the company. I am sorry to see a company that had so many great, hard-working employees and a solid reputation taking such a hit. As for me, I figure it was a 'speed bump' in my career, and the skills and experience that I bring from that company will serve me well in spite of the way it turned out."

- "It's been very difficult for the last couple of years after the problems with the company hit the media. I was really hoping that it would turn around because I believed in the company and enjoyed the work that I was doing there, but it hasn't happened. So I am ready to move forward knowing that even though the company had problems, I had a good work experience where I learned valuable skills such as how to do more with less. I can bring that skill to my next company."

"Give me an example of a time when your integrity was tested."

■ "When I was working in the human resources department on a computer project, we knew how to access salary information. My partner on the project printed out the information and gave it to me. I told him I wanted nothing to do with it. He proceeded to take the information and share it with other team members. I was called in by the vice president of human resources a few days later and was questioned about the information. I told him that I never looked at it and had nothing to do with the sharing. I was asked if I knew that my partner had printed out copies, and I said yes. There was a hearing about the incident, and I had to give my input although I didn't like doing it since my partner was in trouble. Unfortunately he was fired. I felt bad for him but knew that I had done the right thing."

■ "While doing taxes for one of the companies that I worked for, I was asked to do something that would have saved the company several thousands of dollars. I knew that what they were asking me to do was not legal, and, if we were ever audited, I would be questioned and liable. I refused on the grounds that I could not risk my status and license. My boss was not happy with me, but he realized he was doing something that was very high risk. In the end he decided to bite the bullet and go with the legal way of processing the information."

■ "At the bank I worked for, I was asked to process mortgage information for a young couple applying for a loan. I did the calculation and had the figures ready. In the meantime I did some thinking about another way I could do the calculation that would save them percentage points

➡

and a great deal of money. My dilemma was that the bank would make less money on the second calculation. I went to my boss, and he and I looked at the figures together. To my relief, he agreed with me to present the figures saving the couple the money. In the long run the couple returned many times to finance other purchases over the years. We had won their customer loyalty with our honesty."

"Your previous company went bankrupt. How involved were you with the budgeting process?"

- "I worked in the accounting department, so I did see bills that were overdue and late notices and calls from vendors, but that was pretty much the extent that I was aware of what was happening. It was very disappointing to see such a hard-working company have to resort to bankruptcy."
- "As a human resources specialist I was aware of budget problems and plans to restructure the spending, but I had no input into the decisions that were made and the actions taken. I could only do my part with my own department spending and budget. It came as a surprise that the company had to file for bankruptcy."
- "The bankruptcy was inevitable with the amount of spending taking place compared to the amount of money coming in. I didn't have any power in policy matters, but there were several cost-saving measures that could have been taken long before it was necessary to file for bankruptcy."

Problems with a Previous Boss

"Tell me about a boss you didn't get along with."

- "Unfortunately, I did have a problem with my boss and my being assertive in one of my jobs. He was in the habit of talking loudly when he took personal calls, and he sometimes used inappropriate language for the office. Because he was the boss, most of the employees just tried to turn a deaf ear. But one day I happened to be in his office, and we were discussing morale. I took the opportunity to tell him that I had a problem with his personal calls and language. He was really taken aback both that I had brought it up and that anyone was offended by what he was saying. He knew he was in the wrong and changed his behavior after that."

- "My boss and I have very different personalities, and we recognize that. There have been some times when we didn't agree, but agreed to disagree. It wasn't that I challenged him. It was that I sometimes saw an easier solution to a problem. I think we actually enjoyed our 'sparring' times. One thing I can tell you, and he would tell you as well, is that we always treated each other as professionals and respected each other's point of view."

- "There are some problems that just can't get worked out. I always try everything possible, but part of knowing when to give up is a matter of skill and judgment. My current boss and I just don't seem to mesh. He didn't select me as his administrative assistant. He inherited me as the result of a reorganization. I think he would have chosen a less assertive person who wasn't as independent as I am. My independence has allowed me to make sound judgments when I worked for bosses who wanted me to operate that way. I can work with minimal supervision, but I am also a very strong team player and prefer working with supportive teams."

"Have you ever had problems so severe with management that you resigned?"

- "Yes, there were problems at one of the companies that I worked for that caused me to resign. I would prefer not to discuss the details because it is proprietary information that I am talking about, but there were some ethical issues that I had concerns about. I have a high work standard and consider myself a very honest person who chooses not to work with companies that don't have the same values."

- "There was some unprofessional behavior by management at my last company that caused me to resign. I prefer not to say anything against an individual and especially management, but there are labor laws that I feel obliged to uphold, and management felt it could bend the laws slightly. I decided it was in my best interest to resign."

- "I didn't resign, but I also didn't approve of some of the decisions made regarding the payment of overtime in certain situations. I made sure that I was following the law or at least documenting that I had informed the manager of the law so that it was his decision whether he wanted to follow the rules or not. In retrospect, I think I should have resigned when I felt uncomfortable, but I liked the company and the people so I stayed."

"What do you do when you have an irresolvable conflict with your supervisor?"

- "I've never had that happen, but if I did, I would try to talk to the supervisor in a nonaccusatory manner. I try to deal with problems before they get too big and out of control. This way of handling situations has helped me get along with people whom I work with whether they are my bosses or coworkers."

- "The first thing I do is to try to look at the problem or conflict from all sides. I know that there are always two sides to every disagreement. Then I decide whether this 'battle' is worth losing 'the war' over. In other words, I have to work with this supervisor who has power over my work, and so I have to decide whether it is a matter worth pursuing to the next level of management or human resources or whether it is a matter that should just be forgotten. I then take appropriate action."

- "I have always been taught that the boss is the person in charge and have always shown respect for the position. If, however, the conflict involved something that was a morale or legal issue, then I would have to go to the next level of authority with the problem. I have been fortunate to have supervisors whom I have gotten along well with in my career. I have never had to take anything to that extreme."

Lacking Experience

"Judging from your résumé and your years of experience, I am in doubt that you will be able to step up to this job. What makes you think that you can do the job?"

- "I provided technical problem resolution and ensured effective coordination of activities in every job that I have held. I have also gained a reputation within the manufacturing industry as being a key player when it comes to hard bargaining and negotiations. In my last two jobs I was able to save the companies thousands of dollars through savvy business deals."

- "One of my strengths is being able to explain complicated financial reports to nonfinancial people. I presented a report to a group of managers and executives on a very complicated tax issue. Through my Powerpoint presentation of charts and graphs and my ability to break down the information into everyday terminology, I was able to explain in detail what this situation meant to the future of the company. I was commended on my presentation and for making it easy to understand."

- "My successes in customer service have made me one of the top producers in my company. I have customers who ask for me specifically when they have problems because they know that I will listen and do whatever I can to resolve the problem."

"I notice that you are changing fields. What can you bring to this position from your previous career?"

- "I had to deal with a diversity of customers in my last job, and that is the common denominator in these two jobs. I've had some very angry customers to deal with in my job as a customer service rep. Those situations are very difficult to handle because we try to make the customer 'right.' Some people can get downright nasty. I have been in the business long enough to know that I can't take it personally, but it still doesn't feel good when I can't resolve a problem. This is the skill that would get me through the transition to this new field."

- "I have worked effectively in three different industries and have been able to make the transition with minimal downtime to learn. My ability to learn quickly and 'hit the ground running' has made a huge impact on my career."

- "There are some skills that I feel transfer to any job I do. Those are some of my strongest skills. I have excellent communication skills and am fluent in Spanish and English. I have a great rapport with internal and external customers. People who have worked with me know that they can come to me with any issues—business or personal. I'm a great listener and really care about people. My attitude is a personal trait that I feel has gotten me through many a tough situation. I am calm under pressure and will do whatever it takes to get the job completed."

"Give me an example of working with diverse groups of people, including those with less experience."

- "One of my strongest skills is my ability to work with a diversity of people. Regardless of the situation, I have the ability to adapt and work under whatever the circumstances may be. In my last job I worked in a small room with 13 people all speaking various languages, and I still managed to stay focused. No matter whom I work with, I treat them as a professional and if I can help them, I will go out of my way to do so."

- "I think one of the more challenging aspects of today's workplace is that there is a diversity of people—all ages, cultures, and levels of experience. I am very aware that there are many feelings involved, and everyone has to respect the role and the space of coworkers. There was a time when a young woman became very upset. She cleared her desk onto the floor and jumped up on top of the desk and started stomping her feet. I stayed calm and eventually talked her down and out of the building as quickly as I possibly could. She had her feelings hurt by a coworker and didn't know how to handle her feelings. Those are the types of problems I can handle because of my maturity and my easy-going style."

- "One of the skills that I take pride in is my ability to listen to people and really hear what they say. I consider this to be key in dealing with people at any age or stage. I was able to help a young man through a very challenging period of his career by becoming his mentor. I have a very patient style and like to teach by explaining with very concrete examples. The young man I helped is now one of the top producers in the department and is very grateful to me for helping him lay the foundation for his career."

"What has been your experience with taking risks in your job?"

- "One of my jobs in mergers and acquisitions was to research and analyze risks and benefits of possible deals. I discovered some high-risk factors while researching one company and could not recommend the deal based on my findings. I knew that my manager wanted this particular deal to go through and that she wouldn't be happy with my findings. I put together the facts and figures on spread-sheets and made a presentation to her. Although disappointed, she trusted my work and was satisfied that I had exhibited due diligence in getting the facts needed."

- "One example of taking a risk and trying something new is when I was able to lead a cross-functional team in a company that had never used cross-functional teams before. As the lead engineer I decided to try an experiment and took people from various functions and cross-trained them. It was a huge success, and production doubled in a month. The employees really accepted it because it made them feel like they were learning something new that would be of value to them in future jobs. It was received well by management and is now a common practice at the company."

- "There is always a risk when analyzing data and breaking it down so that the customer can understand the facts. I did this for a man who was having a difficult time understanding the numbers and was refusing to buy until he did. I ran several compilations for him—some which was not the usual information we share. I thought in this case it would

➡

benefit the sale if he could understand all the data. I spent extra time with him until he was he able to recognize the benefit that we offered. I took a risk of putting in extra effort, and it paid off."

"Have you ever not taken a risk and later regretted it?"

- "On the personal side I would tell you that I made some investments that I wish that I hadn't, but nothing of that nature at work. I play it pretty conservative at work."
- "I took a risk by taking a new job that I wasn't really ready for. It was an 'acting supervisor job.' In the beginning, I have to admit I struggled with the position. When they offered it to me as a regular position, I should have said, no, but I was afraid I would get passed over the next time. I took the job and eventually ended up being laid off. That job was not for me, and I knew it. I should have trusted my instincts."
- "I have many regrets in my career, but I consider them all learning experiences. One risk I took was taking a job selling a product that I did not believe would work. Well, it didn't, and I ended up feeling bad about all the people I had sold it to. I am an ethical person who really has to believe in the product that I am selling."

"Tell me about the most successful risk you've taken."

- "I didn't feel I was ready to take on added responsibility in my last job. My boss was a great mentor and coach and encouraged me to try the new tasks. They involved working with the international team, and I was intimidated because of my lack of exposure to the global picture. It turned out that my interpersonal skills allowed me to bond quickly and make friends almost from the start. Not only was it a successful undertaking, but it allowed me to take a new direction in my career path."

- "I accepted a job in another state where I didn't know a soul. I was nervous about the job and the transition to a new place to live. The job turned out to be wonderful, and among the people I met was my future wife. If I hadn't taken the risk of venturing into a new situation, I would have never had the opportunities I have had in my business life as well as my new personal life."

- "I joined a start-up company as one of the first ten employees. I knew that it could go either way. I could make some money on my stock options, or I could be out of a job rather quickly. It turned out to be the most fun and challenging work experience of my life. We didn't get rich, but we all did well by taking the risk of being first."

Physical Disabilities

"Is there any reason that you cannot perform the duties of this job with reasonable accommodation?"

- "I have read the job posting and description and have all the necessary skills and then some to perform the duties of the job. I would need accommodation with the computer screen. My vision is such that I need a magnifier that is easily purchased and installed so that I can work for long periods of time without my eyes getting irritated. My previous employers have been able to accommodate my needs and have found it worth the effort because of my extensive knowledge and strong ability to work with accounting data and systems."

- "As you can see from my résumé, I have strong computer skills and customer service experience. The fact that I am in a wheelchair would require a ramp to provide me with access to the building. I noticed that you had such a ramp in place, so there shouldn't be any problem for me to get in and out of the building. I have an excellent reputation for my dependability, reliability, and punctuality. I can't remember a single time when I was late for work."

- "According to your job posting, it is requirement of the job to be able to lift up to 35 pounds. Could you tell me how often lifting would be required? If it were a small percentage, I wouldn't have a problem with the responsibility. If it were a major part of the job, then I would need assistance with the lifting requirement. I have been able to lift at my last jobs with no problem. In fact if you asked my last boss, she would tell you that I am a ball of energy, and I do not let challenges slow me down. I can

➡

be very resourceful about getting around problems I encounter."

"I see you are in a wheelchair. How will that affect your ability to do this job?"

- "The way I look at it is that I bring my own chair. I have done data entry without a problem for over eight years. If you check with the people I've listed as my references, they will tell you that I am efficient and accurate and that my wheelchair does not affect my work or my ability."

- "The only problem that I have ever experienced in my ten years of working in this industry is when the aisles are too narrow. But that is rare in a business environment where there are buildings that comply with OSHA codes and standards."

- "It's not a problem for me or my performance. Sometimes people have to get used to my being in a wheelchair, but I figure that is their problem. Most people tell me after they get to know me that the wheelchair is so much a part of me that after a while they don't even notice there is one."

"What is the greatest challenge you encounter with your disability at work?"

- "My biggest challenge is with people getting used to my being blind. After a while they are amazed at how well I can get around and how I observe things that they do not. Once they accept me, they forget that I can't see what they can."

- "People are very reluctant to shake hands with a hook. When I put my 'hand' out to shake hands, some people draw back. But my attitude soon puts them at ease.

I guess they figure that if I am okay with it, they are too. I have had very few problems performing at top level in all of my previous jobs."

- "I think attitude is the biggest challenge working with people whether you have a disability or not. If you asked all the people who have ever worked with me, they would tell you that I have one of the most upbeat attitudes of any one they know. Some people have told me that I inspire them when they get down and feel sorry for themselves. I don't feel sorry for myself, I am grateful for each day and live it to the fullest."

"I noticed on your reference sheet that your last boss is not listed. Is there any reason for this?"

- "I would prefer that you not contact my last boss because I don't think she can supply an accurate reference for me. She was brought in six months ago to replace my boss who went on maternity leave. My boss who was on maternity leave and I had a unique partnership in our work together. Unfortunately, she decided to quit her job and stay home with her baby. The temporary boss was offered the job, and I don't feel she really ever got to understand my role. In fact, my role was entirely different with her from what it was with my last boss. My last boss would tell you that I was her 'right-hand man.'"

- "Yes, I prefer that none of the people at my last job be contacted. My experience there was not a pleasant one. The people I worked with were very nice and a good team to work with, but management was less professional than at other places I have worked. I know that anyone who worked with me or has managed me in the past would be glad to tell you how adaptable and resourceful I am."

- "My current boss does not know that I am planning to leave the company. Unfortunately, I have gone as far as I can go at my current company, and I want to make a proactive move before I get bogged down and no longer have cutting-edge skills. I have been taking classes in the evening and want to apply what I have learned and join a dynamic team such as the one at this company. If you were to talk to my boss, he would tell you that I am very ambitious and goal-oriented. He would also tell you that he has praised me and promoted me to where I am today."

"We will be doing a background check that includes a credit check. Do you have any problem with that?"

- "I am going to tell you before you see for yourself that I did have a time in my life when my credit was not sterling. It was a time when I was going through a nasty divorce, and it has taken me the last five years to clear up my credit record. I am proud to say that I have been an on-time bill payer since that period ended."
- "I am a person who has high integrity, and any marks you will see on my credit rating are due to hitting some exceptional spending times in my life. Overall my credit has been excellent. There was a time when we were buying a house and furniture that we got in over our heads. We are very conscientious about paying our bills on time and working on being debt-free. I pride myself on my ability to manage money at home and at work. I have always come in under budget on projects that I have overseen in my work."
- "The downturn in the economy has caught my husband and me offguard, and we have not been proud of our credit rating. When my husband and I were laid off at the same time, it was tough to meet all the payments on time. I am proud to say that by writing to the creditors, we were able to negotiate a more lenient payment plan. We are very careful to pay bills on time, even if it is not the full amount due. Things are turning around. My husband has a great new job, and I am confident that I am going to get a great job. We are in the process of pulling resources together to get our feet back on the ground. Neither of us wants to be

in debt to anybody, except maybe the mortgage broker. It will be a while before the mortgage is paid off."

"You didn't provide any references on your job application. What is the reason for this?"

■ "I have a separate sheet for references. If you would like that sheet, I would be glad to provide it. I prefer to give the names of references after I have an interview to ensure that these people are called only when there is a potential job at hand."

■ "When we are sure that we are both in a position to decide whether I will be a candidate for this job, I will be glad to give you references. I feel references are confidential information to be given out when the time is appropriate. I would not want my references to be unnecessarily contacted."

■ "I use a variety of references for different positions, depending on what the job content is. The reason for doing this is that for more technical jobs I think it is appropriate to talk to a technical person. When the position is more people-oriented, I think it is appropriate to talk to persons who have seen me work in that capacity. I will be glad to provide my references when we agree what the job responsibilities are."

Salary

"What do you expect in the way of salary for this position?"

- "I really need more information about the position before I can begin to discuss salary. Can you tell me the range budgeted for this position?"
- "What do you typically pay someone with my experience and education in this type of position?"
- "I'm sure when the time comes and I know more about the facts of the position and how it fits into the bigger picture, we can come to a mutually agreeable figure."

"Can you name a salary range that you would require to take this job?

- "From the research that I have done it appears to be in the $60–70,000 range. Is that the range you had in mind?"
- "Based on my previous experience and education and the 'going rate' for this type of position, I would like to be in the mid to high 70s. Is that a range that fits with your compensation structure?"
- "I would need to know more about your salary structure and how often you review salaries as well as your entire package before I could discuss salary ranges. Could you provide me with more information before we discuss this subject?"

"Would you consider taking less pay than you made in your last job?"

- "I would really need to know more about the opportunity and your whole package before I can give you an answer to that question. My last job had extra perks that this job may not have. Basically, I need more information before I decide."

- "While my highest career value is not money, it is important to me that I be fairly compensated for the work I do. I would be willing to listen to a fair offer based on what I bring to the position in the way of experience and education."

- "Opportunity is valuable to me, so I am always willing to look at the bigger picture. I would always want to be paid according to what I bring to the position, but would be willing to be somewhat flexible when it comes to dollars."

Part Three

**Perfect Phrases for
the Perfect Interview:
Special Types of Jobs**

Chapter Five

Perfect Phrases for Executive Management

The higher the level of responsibility, the more detail and examples will be required to demonstrate your ability and accomplishments. Being specific as possible with your examples through stories of your experiences will add to the credibility of your statements.

Leadership

"What was your leadership role in your last company?"

- "In every job I have assumed more responsibility with success. My last position was as general manager of the entire East Coast operation. I built and led new business units, that resulted in lower expenditures and greater returns on investment. My strength lies in my interpersonal relations. I learned early in the game that people are the cornerstone of success, and I am always sure to give credit where credit is due."

- "As national sales operations manager I trained, developed, and lead a 15-person national account sales and support team targeting hospital accounts worldwide. I also provided strategic and tactical leadership and successful technology installations."

- "As CEO of a retail chain I was in full charge of strategic planning and operations. I also had distribution and profit-and-loss responsibility under my management. I led the operation to accelerated growth and nationwide expansion."

Management Style

"How would you describe your style of managing people?"

- "My management style is to lead by example as a catalyst, and role model in achieving results through others. I make an effort to be visible and involved with employees, letting them know that I am available and willing to help in any-way that I can."

- "As a manager who came up through the ranks of this company, I keep those who need to know informed and up-to-date with relevant and useful information. I stay par-ticularly close to the sales representatives who are out there selling the company and the product. I see them as the basic foundation of keeping the company afloat."

- "I believe in the development of those working in any capacity in the company. By offering learning and continu-ous growth opportunities, I have seen more employee loy-alty and motivation. I believe every employee should feel he or she is making a contribution to the bigger picture and that there are opportunities for growth with the company."

Keeping Abreast of Current Business

"There have been a great many changes in this industry in the past year. How have you kept up with the latest industry news?"

■ "Every day I take time to read journals and newspapers. I guess you could call me a 'newshound.' I also have an excellent memory for detail and can sometimes relate something that I read to an event that occurred months ago. I make sure that I am up-to-date with industry news."

■ "I find the Internet to be the most valuable tool out there. It's very easy to keep up with what's new, and I can do it on my own time. I'm a night owl and am often on the computer into the wee hours of the morning reading up on the latest trends and issues."

■ "Between the TV and radio news and reading various newspapers and journals, I keep up to date on the industry as well as the world news. Globalization makes it necessary to reach beyond local issues. I spend a great deal of time in my car and always listen to news programs on the radio. Those shows allow me to hear snippets of news that I can follow up on the Internet in the evening."

Financial Savvy

"Tell me about a time when your knowledge of finance and business operations made a difference in the company's profits."

- "The key staff members of the last company I worked for all agreed and were committed to a goal of increasing profits 20 percent by the end of the fiscal year. As the CFO I met with the executive team, and we set very specific goals to accomplish this. I was able to get the commitment of individual team members, and we agreed they would receive a percentage of profits at the end of the year if things went as planned. I personally was committed and held accountable to the board of directors. We worked as a team to achieve a very successful campaign rollout. The key was to keep our specific goals in mind and to also keep in continuous communication with one another on the progress of our projects. As it turned out, we exceeded our goal, and every one of us benefited from the team effort."

- "One of the projects that I was most proud of at my last company was the streamlining and enhancing of the corporate budgeting process. I was able to analyze the company's needs and processes and to benchmark activities. The realigning made the process the cornerstone of the way the company's operations are currently measured."

- "When I joined my current company, all the accounting and payroll functions were outsourced. This was not only cumbersome to manage, but also very expensive. By developing and implementing appropriate internal

141

policies and procedures, I was able to convince management to bring the functions back in-house. The overall savings was over 40 percent of what had been spent in a six-month period."

The Big Picture

"How do you manage others day-to-day while focusing on the big picture?"

- "By setting key objectives within the larger organizational context, I am able to stay focused and on top of the management of projects while still maintaining the team's trust. I don't think you'd find anyone that I have ever worked with who would say that I 'micromanage.' I believe in helping others maintain their focus and avoiding 'analysis paralysis,' I have been successful in moving projects forward while not taking away from the leadership of the project."

- "I pride myself on making decisions only after I have considered the 'bigger picture.' That is to say, I am very aware of how the pieces fit together while working with individual team members. Each member of the team plays a part in the success of a project, and I encourage each person to stay focused on the 'whole' project, whether it's a customer's need or a long-term goal. I believe that my open communication style has contributed greatly to my success in managing people."

- "My approach to marketing involves retaining current customers first, and attracting new customers second. One challenge I have faced is customer retention. I work with my staff and members of other relevant departments to retain first, build second. One method that has worked in the past is to send teams to interview 'the customer.' By feeding the data collected to the marketing department, we used 'permission marketing'—ask first, send only upon request for information. The success of a program is our working together as a team to support any campaign from the beginning."

Chapter Six

Perfect Phrases for Managers

Whenever a question begins with a specific request such as "Tell me about a time," or "Can you give me an example... ," the answer will require that you relate a specific incident in which you performed an action.

The formula for a strong story is to tell the interviewer— **"Why you did it," "What you did,"** and **"What the outcome was."** In other words, the story needs a beginning, a middle, and an end.

Tip—Remember to listen to the question and determine if the interviewer is asking for **"a"** time or **"an"** example and, if so, then answer the question with a specific example.

Decision Making

"Tell me about a time when you had to make a decision that you knew would be unpopular."

■ "I consider myself a strong manager who is open to suggestions. I had one experience in which I had to make a decision that was not well accepted by my staff. It involved cutting one of the benefits they were receiving. I had a meeting and announced the news to the staff. It was greeted with a great deal of anger and frustration. I listened and addressed every question that was asked of me. I had done my research and homework and was able to use facts to demonstrate that the cost-benefit ratio was not in line with good business decisions. They left less upset than when they first heard the news, but it took some time for the bad feelings to go away completely. I believe that talking with them intelligently and using facts made a difference in their feelings in the long run."

■ "There was a time when I hired a manager from outside the organization. This was met with hard feelings by some of the contenders for the job who had been passed over. I took a hard stand, even though it was not a popular one. I talked to the disgruntled individuals one-on-one and tried to explain my reasons. Although it is not my preferred style, I had to exercise my authority here. I have to admit there were some tense days to live through at that time, but I firmly believed that I knew what was best for the long haul, and it turned out I was right."

■ "As part of management, I realize that my decisions will not always be viewed as positive. One of those times was when I had to make a quick decision to buy advertising at a spe-

146

cial rate in order to achieve a quick roll out of a time-sensitive product. I had analyzed the budget and was attempting to gain maximum leverage. I was later criticized for not having consulted the team and getting input. My decision was made based on getting the most value for the least amount of money. Fortunately for me, the project rolled out in a timely manner and was quite successful."

Delegation

"How do you manage through delegation?"

- "At my last company, I had the responsibility of setting standards for the group and for being a role model for the other managers. While others gave appreciated input, it was ultimately my job to meet the goals. I set the course of direction and then made sure the other managers and supervisors were onboard with me. My management style is to let each manager run his or her department as a small business. I stayed in touch through one-on-one and group meetings and by making myself available to deal with issues and problems as needed. Although I led the team, the team itself accomplished the goals."

- "Deadlines are a way of life in my business. We had a publication deadline, and it was not a choice between quality and making the deadline. We had to produce both. I brought in some outside production editors to make sure that the team members weren't stretched so tight that they were making major errors. We made the deadline, and no one ever knew that we almost killed ourselves to do it. I rewarded each team member with a night on the town."

- "One thing I learned early in my career is that no one person makes a project successful. I may lead my team toward the bigger picture or goal, but it is the individual team members who carry out the implementation of the project. My strong communication and organizational skills keep the project on track and moving in the right direction, but ultimately it is my ability to motivate and coach the team members that has made me a successful manager."

Motivating Others

"Tell me about a time when you motivated a team in a unique way."

- "I am a manager who recognizes and rewards hard work. I had a team who came to the rescue with a project that required three months of overtime—weekends and evenings. I made sure that all members of the team talked to me about their family situation and whether it was causing a strain and what they were doing about having some fun outside of work. I rewarded each person with a certificate for a weekend away at a local beach resort when the project ended successfully. I believe in life balance, and I think that is the reason the turnover rate at this company is several digits below the average."

- "As a manager of a customer service team, I have found that competition motivates the employees and they have fun competing. I have set it up so that they earn points for meeting certain goals or plateaus. At the end of the month they cash in the points for merchandise from the 'company store' or for things like movie tickets or dinner coupons. The morale in the department stays high, and there is a great deal of camaraderie relating to these contests."

- "In the sales industry it is very common to have ceremonies to reward top performers. I had been on the receiving end of such rewards when I was a sales rep and found that after a while I had a whole bookshelf full of beautiful trophies that weren't doing anybody any good. When I became the person in charge of selecting awards, I came up with a unique idea to give engraved golf clubs, watches, or luggage as the awards. It was a big change from tradition, but most people were really motivated by a more practical gift. We had a wonderful year that year, and a lot of people walked away with some great gifts."

Communication Style

"Tell me about a time when your communication style influenced a decision."

- "I was the key contact during the labor negotiations of a contract dispute. As the leader of the negotiations in one particular case I was able to let the opposing side know that I heard its issues and that we were trying to accomplish a compromise. At the same time, we weren't willing to give in completely on some of the key points. Because they saw that I was being open, they trusted me and talked to me openly. In the end we were able to satisfy both sides."

- "I am an experienced presenter and often make presentations to groups of major decision makers. There was a particular time that I spoke to key decision makers in a multimillion dollar investment firm. By finding out what their expectations and needs were in the beginning and letting them know that I understood their expectations, I was able to influence them to buy our entire system."

- "I find the key to successful communications and sales is to see the problem from the customer's point of view. I had a customer who did not think he needed my product. He was only going to hear me out because he liked me. I began by asking him about his business, and once I started questioning him, I found out that he would benefit greatly from the product. I spent almost four hours talking to him about his business and what we could do for him. The problem was that no one had taken the time to listen to his needs. People just started selling to him. I ended up with a good customer as a result of listening."

Ability to Influence Others

"Tell me about a time when you were able to convince others that you had a better idea or way of doing things."

- "I worked with a team of product development people to come up with a new product. I was the liaison between the marketing and product development teams. The ideas had to be communicated back and forth between groups. I was the person who had to come up with creative ideas to appease both groups while not offending egos. It was the most challenging project I've ever worked, on but it was also one of the most successful. We were able to come up with a winning product and a successful campaign launch."

- "While working as a project manager, I analyzed the latest data provided and found a flaw in our system. I put together a spreadsheet and presented it to management as well as to my team. I was able to demonstrate what needed to be changed and to justify the cost involved. My team backed my findings, and I was able to influence management to agree to put in a new system at great cost but that in the end would show excellent savings."

- "My writing ability has allowed me to present the facts, but it also gives me an opportunity to present ideas within my own framework. I worked with a team of graphic designers to come up with the Web site for our company. Although the design was very important, the words I wrote blended to make a complete message. The site has been recognized as a top Web site in the industry."

Chapter Seven

Perfect Phrases for Supervisors

D emonstrating leadership qualities during the interview will be necessary if you have had responsiblity for supervising others' work. You should be prepared to talk about how you have related to people and handled people-problems to show your competence in this area.

Supervising Others

"What would your coworkers and subordinates say about your management style?"

- "They would tell you that although I am a manager, I am also the type of person that can be counted on no matter what. They know that they can trust me to keep confidential information confidential and to listen to their problems without repeating them."
- "They would tell you that I would never ask them to do something that I wouldn't do myself. I am not above jumping in and helping when the situation requires it."
- "I require results from my team. My team members would tell you that every member is aware and focused on the objectives and outcome of the project as a whole and not as individual contributors. They would also tell you that I am fully committed to the team effort."

Handling Personnel Problems

"Give me an example of a time when you had to handle a personnel problem and what you did."

- "One of the people I supervised was not following the protocol for making requests. I asked him politely to use the forms that everyone else was using, but he became belligerent. I took him aside when the opportunity presented itself and told him that he and I needed to have an understanding so that we could work things out. He knew that I would eventually have to take the problem to the next level and decided it was in his best interest to cooperate. There were no further problems after that, and from then on he followed procedure and acted professionally toward me and the other team members."

- "I had a difficult problem with a supervisor who was taking credit for the work that her team accomplished. Some of the team members came to me and complained. They said it was affecting their attitude. I called the woman in and explained how her taking credit was affecting production and morale. She became very upset that others saw her that way, and she said she was unaware of her behavior or the reactions of others. She wanted my advice as to how to change the situation, and I suggested talking to each person about how much she appreciated his or her team effort. She took my advice, and there was a noticeable improvement in morale as well as in her behavior after that."

- "Selling the concept of change when merging companies has been one of my greatest challenges. When a company of a similar size acquired my current company, it seemed like everyone wanted to be unhappy and complain. By holding a series of meetings with the people affected, I was able to start them looking at the positives of the situation—a stronger team, more exposure in the market, better benefits, etc. Eventually they did begin to see it from the other point of view, but it was a tough sale."

Follow-Through

"You say that one of your strengths is follow-through. When has that made a difference in your work?"

- "As a pharmaceutical sales rep if I didn't follow through on my promises, I couldn't have survived. I remember there was one doctor who wasn't going to see me or to buy my product no matter what I did. My first strategy was to get past the office manager, who I call 'the gatekeeper.' I went in once a week and chatted with her and said that I was just following through. Eventually I found out that she liked music, and that gave me something to discuss with her. If she told me she was attending a concert or music event, I went out of my way to ask how it was on my next visit. I think she finally decided I was an okay-kind-of-guy, and she was able to get me in to see the doctor. She told me that I was the first sales person to show any interest in her or the workings of the office. When I did get to meet the doctor, I used the same approach on him, finding out what his interests were. It worked like a charm. I was able to sell the most product this doctor had ever bought from the company."

- "As a human resources supervisor I have to constantly follow through on details of projects for managers. It seems as though everything happens at the end of the year regarding performance reviews and raises. Last year we had a mandatory holiday break, and the data for raises to be effective January 1st had to be submitted two weeks earlier than usual. If you've worked with managers who dreaded completing their performance reviews you will know what I am talking about when I say it can be 'like

➥

pulling teeth.' I was working with two managers who were behind schedule, and I didn't seem to be able to make any progress. I finally made a deal with them. If they would send two a day for a week, we could complete the project on time. Each morning I would call and ask if there was anything I could do to help them make the daily quota. It got so they looked forward to my call and my reminder. I am proud to say that I made that deadline, and the managers actually thanked me for getting them through their dreaded chore."

- "I remember a project on which I supervised seven people. Between the multiple projects going on and the seven people to keep track of, I wouldn't have survived without being very organized with reminders to myself to follow through on certain dates, projects, or upcoming events. My work ethic is that if I say I am going to do something, I can assure you that I will do it, if at all possible. This project was no exception. It was on time with only a minor problem or two to take care of along the way."

Initiating

"Tell me about a time when you initiated an action that brought results."

- "I am a person who tries to plan ahead, and so I usually have a planned schedule for every step of a project. There was a time however when my plan started to fall apart because of a systems crash. It was chaotic for a while until I called and located office space that wasn't being used for a few days. I was able to bring my team into the space and utilize the equipment needed to complete the job. We were back on schedule in no time and met the deadline."

- "As a project manager for my last company I could see a need for a template to guide team members through projects while allowing them to prioritize. I came up with a prototype and presented it to my manager. She liked the idea and suggested I follow through on the development. I did some refining based on her suggestions and then presented it to my team. Members were delighted to have a format to assist them in organizing their tasks. After the template was put in place and used successfully, my boss presented it to management and they okayed it to be used companywide. I received an award for not only the idea but for initiating a more efficient process that will save time and ultimately money."

- "As an officer in the military I had many occasions to initiate action. One time in particular there was a plan of action that went bad, and I had to step in and take the initiative and make a very quick decision. We were in a live fire exercise that should have stopped when a signal was fired. I shot the signal flare, but the firing didn't stop. I had to make a decision and had my troops hit the deck. I then signaled to the radioman to call in a cease-fire. All fire stopped immediately, and all troops were reported safe. I found out later that the platoon firing the machine guns never got the message about the cease fire signal and would have just continued firing. My initiative and quick decision saved my troops from being seriously injured or killed that day."

Problem Solving

"Give me an example of a time when your efforts solved a problem."

- "I headed up a project that involved customer service personnel and technicians. I organized a meeting to get everyone's buy-in on a new project that would increase sales opportunities. I held a meeting to brainstorm and get input. One of the problems was that there were technical and nontechnical people involved, and they had different ideas of how the project should run. I drew up a plan, taking the best ideas from both groups and then organized teams, balancing the mixture of technical and nontechnical people. We had a deadline to meet, and I did periodic checks with the teams. After three weeks, we were exceeding expectations, and the team members had a new respect for each other's contributions."

- "One of the most challenging problems I faced as a supervisor was in creating a strategic alliance with a provider of chemicals to use its specialized blending equipment and delivery network. The provider was not interested in a sale because it was such specialty equipment. What I came up with was an exchange. My team would provide marketing, billing, and technical assistance for the use of the equipment. The provider jumped at the opportunity. I convinced my team that this was a win-win situation, and the project moved forward without a hitch."

- "In my last position I faced a challenge of some kind almost every day. One day that stands out was when we had a 'sick out' day when several of the team members called in sick as a protest against an unpopular decision to change their

➡

benefit plan. We were short several key people who were necessary to keep the plant running. I appealed to management for help, and much to my surprise, they volunteered to come forth themselves to run the plant for the day. Some of them had come up through the ranks so it was a bit like 'coming home.' It was a very trying day with so many bosses in one place, but we managed to pull it off. Fortunately the protest only lasted one day."

Part Four

**Final
Preparations**

Chapter Eight

Exercises for the Perfect Phrase

Quiz: Writing Your Own Perfect Phrases

Now it's your turn to try writing "perfect phrases." There are no exact answers. The idea is to see if you can turn a "flawed phrase" into a stronger answer with a "perfect phrase." You will find suggested answers later in the chapter.

1. **What are your goals?**

   Flawed Phrase: "I am seeking a challenging job in a growth-oriented company where I can utilize my skills to the best of my ability."

   Perfect Phrase: _____
   _____
   _____
   _____
   _____

2. Do you have any questions?

Flawed Phrase: "No, you've pretty much covered everything that I wanted to know."

Perfect Phrase:

3. You don't seem to have any experience in this field.

Flawed Phrase: "No, I don't have any experience with that system."

Perfect Phrase:

4. How would your current boss describe you?

Flawed Phrase: "My current boss inherited me and doesn't really know me or what I do. He's gone most of the time and doesn't have time to give me. That's been a problem for me in my job."

Perfect Phrase:

5. **What do you like best about working with your current company?**

   Flawed Phrase: "My current company used to be a great company to work for, but since the merger with the other company, things just aren't the same. I liked it better when we were smaller and had more control over our projects."

   Perfect Phrase:_____

   _____

   _____

   _____

6. **What are your strengths?**

   Flawed Phrase: "My strengths are my ability to get the job done. I'm a hard worker."

   Perfect Phrase:_____

   _____

   _____

   _____

7. **What are your weaknesses?**

   Flawed Phrase: "My weakness is my memory. Sometimes I forget things and have to put little stickies up to remind myself what I have to do."

   Perfect Phrase:_____

   _____

   _____

   _____

8. **What is your salary expectation?**

   Flawed Phrase: "I am currently making $40,000 and would like to receive a 10 to 15 percent increase."

   Perfect Phrase:_____

   _____

   _____

   _____

9. **Why are you leaving your current job?**

   Flawed Phrase: "I have outgrown my current job and am looking for a challenge. I want to grow and develop and learn new things."

   Perfect Phrase:_____

   _____

   _____

   _____

10. **Why do you want to work for this company?**

    Flawed Phrase: "I was searching the Internet for a job and found your posting and thought it would be an interesting and challenging job where I could utilize my skills."

    Perfect Phrase:_____

    _____

    _____

    _____

    _____

ANSWERS

1. What are your goals?

Perfect Phrase: "I like to think of goals in the short and long term. My short-term goal is to find a company that is a good fit for me and the company. Once I begin to be a contributor, I would like to continue to grow and take on more responsibility for projects."

Note: Avoid using phrases that don't really say anything specific. They don't mean anything.

2. Do you have any questions?

Perfect Phrase: "Yes, I do. Could you tell me about the company culture and how the current economy is affecting your business?"

Note: This is your opportunity to find out important information about the company.

3. You don't seem to have any experience in this field.

Perfect Phrase: "My experience is with a system very similar to that one. In fact, I learned to use the system I am currently using within two weeks of starting my job. Because I like computers so much, new things come quickly to me. I can be up and running in record time."

Note: If you don't have experience with something in particular, think of something similar that you picked up very quickly. Let the interviewer know that you will be up and running in no time and that he won't have to hold your hand through the process.

4 . How would your current boss describe you?

Perfect Phrase: "My boss would tell you that I work very independently without a lot of direction. He has had to depend on me to run things as he travels a great deal."

Note: Never make your boss look bad. By putting a positive spin on the way you say something, you can emphasize your strengths rather than your boss's weaknesses.

5 . What do you like best about working with your current company?

Perfect Phrase: "One thing about my company that I really like is the teamwork that is emphasized there. No matter what department I have worked with, there is a sense of partnership and pulling together. That's important to me in my job."

Note: Never bad-mouth a company or person. This reflects badly on you and the company or person you are talking about. The thinking is that someday you will talk about this person or company like that when you leave.

6 . What are your strengths?

Perfect Phrase: "My strengths are my attitude and my flexibility. I am known for my ability to get the job done; done right; and done on time. I do whatever it takes to fulfill my commitment to deliver."

Note : By using the same phrase everybody else uses, your words lose their impact. By making a more definite, stronger statement with some punch, your words are more likely to impress.

7 . What are your weaknesses?

Perfect Phrase: "I usually have a wonderful memory for details, but sometimes when I am in the middle of several tasks, I have to stop and organize myself and prioritize what has to be done. I make lists and do spreadsheets so that I don't miss any anything. This really helps me remember important details as well as the not-so-important details."

Note: Try putting a positive spin on your weakness and tell what you've learned or are learning to improve on a weakness.

8 . What is your salary expectation?

Perfect Phrase: "When the time comes to talk money, I am sure that we will come up with a mutually beneficial amount. Could you tell me the range budgeted for the position?"

Note: The unwritten rule is, "He who mentions money first loses." Let the interviewer bring up the subject and then let him or her be the first to mention the dollar amount, if possible.

9. Why are you leaving your current job?

Perfect Phrase: "I have set some career goals for myself to become part of a bigger team in the area of negotiations where I can contribute based on my past experiences."

Note: Words and phrases such as, "looking for a challenge," or "to grow and develop and learn new things," are overused and meaningless to the interviewer.

10. Why do you want to work for this company?

Perfect Phrase: "My goal today is to find out why I would want to work for your company. I know that I have what it takes to do this job, and from what I have read while researching your company, it looks like a good match. I am here to find out more about the opportunity."

Note: By putting the interview on equal terms in which I am "checking you out" while you are "checking me out," you will have a stronger position in the interview.

Your Position—Your Words

Each industry uses "key words," or "lingo," for specific positions. To learn these words, research your specific industry to determine the most current jargon. By using these words in your interview, you will demonstrate your knowledge of the industry, and the interviewer will look at you as a candidate who knows what he or she is talking about.

Here are some examples of key words for specific jobs/industries:

Engineering process development, quality assurance, testing and failure analysis, field assessment and operations, industrial hygiene, environmental compliance, urban planning

Teaching/Education scholastic standards, academic achievement, curriculum development, lesson plans, college prep, literacy development, dyslexia, academic levels, multicultural, certification, ethics

Human Resources performance management, managed care, headcount, training and development, multidiscipline, efficiency initiatives, expatriate, relocation, competency-based, unions, internal audits

Law briefs, discovery, civil litigation, initiatives, prosecute, reviews, directives, regulations, compliance, mergers and acquisitions, intellectual property, trademark, regulatory compliance

Exec/Management return on investment (ROI), profit and loss statements (P&L), strategic planning, tactical planning and execution, leadership training, business campaigns, growth and expansion, fast track

Sales territory management, quotas, sales producer, sales campaign, gross per unit, renewal rate, team building, cross-functional, sustained revenue, hands-on, emerging markets

Marketing customer relations management (CRM), turn-around, profitability, target market, world class, vision, operating infrastructure, change initiatives, market penetration

Technology information systems management, next-generation products, data mining, online customer support, broadband, turnkey network solutions, customer-driven, prototyping, troubleshooting

These are only a sample of the words you will discover once you begin to make up your own collection of industry words.

Your Position—Your Words: An Exercise

Take time to write down the key words and jargon used in your position and in your industry. This will prepare you for a wide range of questions you'll be asked.

-
-
-
-
-
-
-

Key Words and How to Locate Them

In addition to finding key words through job postings, another source of industry/job words is *The Occupational Information Network* http://online.onetcenter.org/. You will find a complete list of occupation keywords, SOC codes, and job families. This site also lists skills required—basic skills, social skills, experience, and tasks.

Another place to look are books at your local bookstore or library. Two great resources are

Key Words to Nail Your Job Interview by Wendy S. Enelow, Impact Publications

1500 Key Words for $100,000 + Jobs by Wendy S. Enelow, Impact Publications

About the Author

Carole Martin is a professional interviewer and coach. She is also the author of *Boost Your Interview IQ*, selected as one of the top 10 career books of 2004. In addition to having her own business, she has been an interview expert and a contributing writer at Monster.com. Her unique background includes over 15 years of human resources management experience and a Master's degree in Career Management. She has worked in technical and nontechnical industries, in Fortune 500 as well as start-up companies.

She teaches and coaches interviewing skills at two universities: UC Berkeley's Haas School of Business and John F. Kennedy University.

Her work has extended worldwide as she has coached people through one-on-one and group workshops, in person, or by phone. She is an out-placement workshop presenter for individuals who have been laid off from their jobs. She also consults for companies in the San Francisco Bay area, interviewing candidates to find the best person for the job.

Her favorite interview motto is

Preparation=Self Confidence=Successful Interviews=Job Offers

For more information about Carole's services, see her Web site at http://www.interviewcoach.com.

The Right Phrase for
Every Situation...Every Time

Perfect Phrases for Building Strong Teams
Perfect Phrases for Business Letters
Perfect Phrases for Business Proposals and Business Plans
Perfect Phrases for Business School Acceptance
Perfect Phrases for College Application Essays
Perfect Phrases for Cover Letters
Perfect Phrases for Customer Service
Perfect Phrases for Dealing with Difficult People
Perfect Phrases for Dealing with Difficult Situations at Work
Perfect Phrases for Documenting Employee Performance Problems
Perfect Phrases for Executive Presentations
Perfect Phrases for Landlords and Property Managers
Perfect Phrases for Law School Acceptance
Perfect Phrases for Lead Generation
Perfect Phrases for Managers and Supervisors
Perfect Phrases for Managing Your Small Business
Perfect Phrases for Medical School Acceptance
Perfect Phrases for Meetings
Perfect Phrases for Motivating and Rewarding Employees
Perfect Phrases for Negotiating Salary & Job Offers
Perfect Phrases for Perfect Hiring
Perfect Phrases for the Perfect Interview
Perfect Phrases for Performance Reviews
Perfect Phrases for Real Estate Agents & Brokers
Perfect Phrases for Resumes
Perfect Phrases for Sales and Marketing Copy
Perfect Phrases for the Sales Call
Perfect Phrases for Sales Presentations
Perfect Phrases for Setting Performance Goals
Perfect Phrases for Small Business Owners
Perfect Phrases for the TOEFL Speaking and Writing Sections
Perfect Phrases for Writing Company Announcements
Perfect Phrases for Writing Grant Proposals
Perfect Phrases in American Sign Language for Beginners
Perfect Phrases in French for Confident Travel
Perfect Phrases in German for Confident Travel
Perfect Phrases in Italian for Confident Travel
Perfect Phrases in Spanish for Confident Travel to Mexico
Perfect Phrases in Spanish for Construction
Perfect Phrases in Spanish for Gardening and Landscaping

Visit mhprofessional.com/perfectphrases for a complete product listing.

Learn more. Mc Graw Hill Do more.

THE RIGHT PHRASE FOR EVERY SITUATION...EVERY TIME

The all-important job interview—it's your one chance to sell yourself to a potential employer, and you don't want to blow it. You need to use this crucial opportunity to demonstrate your unique skills, creativity, experience, and value in the workplace, and to do this, you need to know exactly what to say to showcase your strengths. Clearly and succinctly, you must let the interviewer know why you are right for the job—and you must be prepared to answer *any* question. *Perfect Phrases for the Perfect Interview* provides a complete arsenal of ready-to-use responses for a wide variety of interview scenarios. With this quick-reference guide, you will learn how to:

- **Break the ice and make a winning impression**

- **Emphasize your skills, experience, and style— and land the job**

- **Handle tough questions with ease—even if you must explain why you were fired**

- **Communicate your salary and career goals**

In a job interview, every word counts. This essential guide includes specific phrases for any question you'll get asked, as well as exercises, problem words to avoid, and key communication secrets that give you the competitive edge and help you get the job.

Carole Martin of TheInterviewCoach.com, a career consulting practice, is the author of *Boost Your Interview IQ*. Her career advice is also available at Monster.com.

ISBN 978-0-07-144982-3
MHID 0-07-144982-5

50995

$9.95 USA

9 780071 449823

Learn more. Do more.

MHPROFESSIONAL.COM

Cover Design: Gary Brumberg